Starting Right,
Staying Strong

Starting Right, Staying Strong

A Guide to Effective Ministry

by

Daniel L. Johnson

THE PILGRIM PRESS
New York

Library of Congress Cataloging in Publication Data

Johnson, Daniel L., 1940–
    Starting right, staying strong.

    Bibliography: p. 91.
    1. Clergy—Office.   2. Pastoral theology.   I. Title.
BV660.2.J55   1983   253'.2   82-22383
ISBN 0-8298-0648-2 (pbk.)

The Pilgrim Press, 132 West 31 Street, New York, NY 10001

Contents

Introduction

The point of entry into the ordained ministry of the church is a crucial time for anyone who, up to that moment, has been a student and must now become a pastor. One role and identity comes to an end and another begins. The purpose of this book is to explore some of the most pressing questions that arise immediately on the transition from seminary to parish. Such questions are not necessarily answered just by the passage of time; pastors other than those who are newcomers continue to wrestle with the issues of this book. Also, most pastors relocate from time to time, and in some ways a new parish is a fresh start that reopens the initial questions of effective ministry. This book gathers together the critical issues of parish ministry, as I see them, and offers some practical suggestions—mostly for beginning pastors but for more experienced pastors as well.

Seminary training, despite all the recent progress of field-based education, cannot simulate the actual reality of being a parish minister. The academic environment is completely different from the parish. One cannot fully know what it is to be a pastor until actually living and working in the vocation full time, and inevitably, at this point, questions arise that could not have been formulated while the new minister was still in seminary. A common opinion held by pastors in their first year or two of ministry is that seminary education is all wrong and should be redesigned to match the reality of parish responsibility. Longer experience in the ministry, however, usually brings the recognition that no amount of curricular redesign will make it possible to prepare a person adequately for a role that cannot be pre-experienced. A good seminary education provides a solid academic base for ministry, but the parish environment itself becomes the next "school," in which learning of another kind commences.

A word about myself is in order. I am a parish minister of the United Church of Christ and chairperson of an association committee on the ministry, writing for other pastors not because I am uniquely qualified to offer advice, but because I am a practicing minister who believes that valuable communication can and should go on between colleagues. In a sense, I wrote this book for myself, wishing it or something like it had been available when I made the transition from seminary to first parish; it might have helped me. Perhaps you and I are sufficiently alike that this book can help you. My experience is in the United Church of Christ, a denomination that braids various strands of connectional and free-church emphases. But many of the issues touched in this book span divergent polities and are of concern regardless of denomination. The experiences of pastors in all the various branches of the church are remarkably similar as one comes to terms with responsible leadership and institutional requirements.

For those who have just completed seminary training

and are getting started in their first parish ministries, this book is offered with the conviction that the wheel need not be constantly reinvented or, to change the metaphor, that strange roads aren't quite so strange when someone who has already traveled them talks with you about them.

Much has been said recently about ministers who leave the ministry for other kinds of work. Sometimes such a decision is realistic and appropriate, but I suspect that often such a move results from unfortunate understandings of ministry and wrong interpretation of its conflicts. My hope is that some of the ideas in this book contribute toward a few decisions to stay in the ministry with renewed intentionality.

Daniel L. Johnson

*Starting Right,
Staying Strong*

1. Getting Started

MOST NEW MINISTERS have their first parish experiences in small, struggling churches that remember better days and favorite pastors long gone. Each denominational system has its own recruitment and placement procedures, ranging from hierarchical to catch-as-catch-can, but regardless of denominational polity and practice, many of these first experiences are remarkably similar.

The people of your parish are the custodians of a personal and particular history and ethos. For some, *guardians* might be a better word. Their memories of this church are sacred memories and therefore ones they will painstakingly protect from alteration. Their gladness at your arrival is mixed with a certain wariness, as they watch and wait to see if you attempt to change things they feel should never change. Your opinion of the sanctuary color or of a particular stained glass window or of the choir repertoire or of the church school curriculum may be sharply different from the opinions held by your parishioners.

As you begin, making an effort to see yourself from the

3

perspective of your parishioners is important. View yourself realistically as building on foundations already established, taking your place somewhere in this church's history to add what you can to its witness and life. Get to know your church's history well. Encourage older members to tell it to you and really listen to them, draw them out. Read the historical documents and study old photographs. Possibly an intricate network of family relationships exists, going back a long way, and your familiarity with these relationships will facilitate your understanding of the congregation. Your parish calling is like a two-way street; you can gain as much from what the people tell you as you can give to them as their new pastor. You cannot build well until you know the strengths and weaknesses in the foundation; such knowledge is not gathered overnight. Take plenty of time to learn, and avoid snap judgments.

Also, get to know your church's place in the community. Most likely, this parish is not in your hometown, and you are a highly conspicuous stranger. But you are welcome as few other kinds of stranger ever are; the people want to like you and want you to like them. You have a unique opportunity to make this your town. You should learn its economic base and income level, its measure of transiency and potential for growth or decline. Do the young people stay or move away? Are new people attracted to relocate here? Statistics available from Washington, DC, the public library, and a detailed map of the area are essential tools. If the town has a historical society, make use of its services. Walk rather than drive whenever possible and really look around. As a pedestrian, your view is quite different from that of a motorist; you have the advantage of being more relaxed, far more perceptive of detail, better able to gauge distances. Introduce yourself to people—shopkeepers, bankers,

4

school authorities, civic leaders, police, hospital personnel, doctors, lawyers. For them to know who you are, on your initiative, is good, but again, you can gain a great deal from their comments to you. Read the local newspaper—every word of it at first—as a valuable discipline. All this, taken together, adds up to a crash course for you, one in which you deliberately set out to make this town *your* town. No matter what the duration of your first pastorate, it will be far more significant if you refuse to think of yourself as transient.

Learn about the other churches in town or nearby and the other ministers. Chapter 8 addresses more specifically your relationship with ordained colleagues, but at first, a friendly call on each of them is time well spent. I had the strange experience of being a new pastor in a town in which almost all the other churches also had new pastors, but more likely you'll be relating to colleagues who know the town well and who see your church from a different perspective than you. Somewhat hidden by social conformity is a distinct class structure that has played an important role in forming and maintaining each of the churches in your town, and the more you know about the values and prejudices built into this class structure, the more you will know about the role your church plays in the sociology of the town. Unfortunately, denominationalism is the cause of much duplication of services and competition; however, each church has its unique specialty or emphasis that adds to the diversity and richness of Christianity. You will be better prepared as a pastor if you look at your church in relation to neighboring churches. One is based on sacramental liturgy; another has developed a fundamentalist ethos; another has a strong young people's program; another is providing support groups; another has some unusually talented members; another may be quietly dying. Instead

5

of each church burning itself up trying to cover all bases, it can interrelate with other churches, resulting in friendly and creative cooperation and mutuality. Much depends on how friendly the various ministers and priests are with one another.

Your primary and most important relationship, of course, is with the people of your congregation. Sometimes you may think of them as being monolithic—a solid, single-minded group—but this is only partly true. Although they have in common the history and ethos of their church, they are far from unanimity on matters of theology, politics, and ideology. The ideological diversity present in all denominations shows up at every level, not the least of which is the local church. Theology ranges from fundamentalist to unitarian. Some of your members are students of the Bible, whereas others are not familiar with the Bible at all and don't care to be. Some want the church to confront social injustice and political problems, whereas others strongly oppose any such involvement. Some see the church as a safe harbor in a confusing world; others see it as a base from which to help make the world safer and less confusing. Some of your members are sophisticated about committee and task force procedures, and others are like bulls in a china shop. If you find such diversity and mixture of values frustrating at first, you ought to know that yours is a normal pastoral reaction. Coming, as you do, from an environment of higher education, in which academic freedom and the presuppositions of liberal education are taken for granted, to a position of relationship and accountability to a local church is more than a little threatening. This is movement across a boundary from one world to another, and it's a culture shock that must be weathered if you are to survive in the ministry. Like any deeply threatening situation, it confronts you with your next major opportunity for growth beyond the seminary level and student identity. Your first responses to this culture shock—be they accommodative and compromising or confrontative and abrasive—will set the tone and pattern of your ministry. Consider the transition you're going through a necessary thrust toward growth and new maturity, not a nasty surprise you wouldn't have encountered in a "better" church. Make good use of your regional denominational executive as you undergo the transition. This is a good habit to acquire right away; you need a pastor too sometimes—someone who has been where you are now and who cares about you and your church.

The transition from seminary to parish is absolutely necessary if the church is to have strong, effective ministers. Some beginning ministers like to return to seminary for refresher courses and for DMn programs and other advanced degrees. If the purpose of such a return is a clear and verifiable strengthening of pastoral skills and effectiveness, this action is certainly to be encouraged. But if the return to campus is experienced as an escape from a locus of unreality to a cherished environment of realism and sophistication, the returning minister is probably better defined as a scholar than a minister. If this is so, a serious problem may be signaled. Scholarship is an essential component of effective ministry, but it is not the main pastoral function or identity. The distinction between student and pastor is crucially important, and the church is best served by clergy who understand and gladly define themselves as pastors first and foremost.

A pastor is not primarily a student or teacher of religion. A student or teacher is most at home in the classroom and library; a pastor may love these places, but they are not "home." *A pastor is a person who uniquely demonstrates the love of God in the life of a specific*

7

congregation. You might want to debate this assertion or modify it. But more and more I find the demonstration of the love of God at the center of what a pastor is all about. Positive energy and creativity, grace, a prophetic edge, and forgiveness need constantly to be channeled through your personality into the life of your church and the individual lives of its members. The difference between the *study* of these qualities and the *living* of them is immense.

At the beginning of your ministry (and, I am finding, throughout my own career) the use of your time is a central issue. (This issue is approached from various angles in subsequent chapters.) In trying to cope with many people's divergent expectations, together with your own agenda for the projects you want to initiate and the needs you want to address, you may find yourself running constantly and inefficiently. This is a perfect predisposition for exhaustion and frustration. Forgetfulness is one symptom of the problem. In my first parish I remember suddenly panicking when a member would say, "See you Thursday night!" and I would draw a blank on where I was supposed to be Thursday night. How helpful it would have been had the person said, "See you Thursday night at the town council meeting," but most people assume you know what they are thinking. The tool most helpful in organizing the use of time and in keeping track of various commitments is a calendar large enough to have date blocks you can write in but small enough to carry with you. I write everything in mine: call so-and-so, write to. . ., lunch with. . ., trustees, prepare Sunday bulletin—everything. A small check beside an entry as soon as I've done it turns the calendar into a valuable diary of items accomplished. It can become a useful resource of data for the writing of regular reports to the church. I would be lost without this tool.

Closely related to how you use your time is the extent to which you train yourself to rely on other people to perform certain tasks. In the past I have said to a parishioner, "*I* will write to so-and-so," when it would have been better for the parishioner's self-esteem and for my own schedule if instead I had said, "Would *you* like to write a letter to so-and-so?" We ministers are not called to *be* the church; we are called to enable and encourage lay persons to be the church. The more we do the tasks that can be done by church members, the more we deprive them of opportunities to gain valuable experience. And given the chance, they can do many things better than you or I. Remember, the more people invest of themselves in the work of the church, the more it is truly their church.

You may or may not have a secretary. If you do, some of your most careful planning should be devoted to how to make the best use of such an employee or volunteer. You might find it helpful to have incoming telephone calls screened; the caller's name and number and the time the call is received are entered in a log. Incoming mail can be handled similarly. Typing is an obvious secretarial function, and a good secretary can even write certain letters, which you need only read and sign. Your appointment calendar may be handled better by a secretary than by you, and someone to remind you of upcoming commitments can be helpful. Also, a secretary can monitor the newspapers for you, clipping items that relate to you or to church members, and can inform you of obituaries of people related to your members. Your secretary may have been associated with the church a long time, and a well-trained memory of family names and relationships is priceless.

A secretary is the best person to handle the printing needs of the church, although here again it may be better ministry to involve lay volunteers in the production of a church newsletter.

These are just a few suggestions for making use of a secretary's skills. By trying to be your own secretary you siphon away valuable energy and time from your primary concentration—the ministry.

How you set up and organize your office also deserves thoughtful planning. If the office is in the church building, sometimes you will wish it were in your home, for quick access and convenience. If you set it up at home, you deprive yourself of a healthy—and sometimes necessary—dividing line between your work and your home privacy. I have tried it both ways. You will need to figure out which is the best method for you. Some ministers need a secret hideaway, where they can prepare sermons and not be interrupted by the telephone and people at the door. Again, a secretary is invaluable when you need to be protected from any interruption for a while. No matter where you decide to locate your office, it serves a two-fold purpose: It is your private study as well as the place in which you will do some pastoral counseling. These two functions are sufficiently different from each other so that two separate rooms might be worth considering.

A desk, for example, is a poor tool in counseling. It creates a barrier between you and those who come to you for help. People will be more comfortable with you in a setting that includes effective room lighting, tasteful furnishings, comfortable and supportive chairs. Your visitor(s) should not have to stare into a lamp in order to see you. Nor should bright window light frame your face or theirs.

A desk, however, is a good tool for your private work. It tells a great deal about you and the way you work. I have to be careful that my desk doesn't become cluttered with letters, memos, notebooks, journals, and books to the point where even I can no longer easily find a certain item. This means a weekly straightening session, in which I am always amazed at how much of what I thought at first was important goes into the wastebasket.

Spend a lot of time, initially, setting up a filing system. Files that hang by side tabs on rails stay much neater than the kind you stuff in a drawer. The extra cost is well worth it. It is wise to buy twice as many file folders as you think you will need, and label one for each committee, organization, and activity in which you participate. Immediately get into the habit of filing materials in the appropriate folders. The problem, of course, with any filing system is that once an item is filed it may well be "out of sight, out of mind." You also need some kind of reminder system that will efficiently keep before you letters requiring answers and materials to bring to someone's attention. Your calendar, a secretary, a bulletin board, an assignment notebook—something other than merely trusting your memory—will come to your aid time and again. A set of 31 numbered manila folders can be used for filing items by "future" dates, so that you are reminded of something requiring attention. This calendar filing system will jog your memory, if you form the habit of looking at what is filed each day for that date. Determine which reminder system is most effective for you, and then build it into your daily living.

Because you are no longer in seminary, where performance and achievement are monitored and evaluated, a natural question is, "How am I doing?" Your parish provides an evaluative feedback that is quite different from that of the academic setting. Many times your best work will go unthanked—but not always. Occasionally, you will be surprised that one of your poorer sermons receives praise. In school you tried to measure up to academic standards, but in the church you attempt to meet a wide range of different and sometimes conflicting expectations. To make sense out of chaos, you would do well, from the beginning, to establish goals for your ministry. A goal is always specific—never a nebulous, subjective quality that can't be measured—for example, to secure a sufficient number of new church school teachers by August 5, to visit every home in the parish by the end of my first year, to have bylaw revisions ready for review by the church council on April 22, to see to it that my church takes a more active role in its association (you may want to substitute a different regional term here). Each of these examples calls for a different subtlety in ministerial leadership, but they are all *measurable*. At the deadline you can tell whether you succeeded or failed. Without such objective data you are adrift in a sea of vague impressions, subjective feedback, and imprecise information. You need to know you're doing a good job, and goal setting is an effective way to discover realistic evaluation. You should almost always engage in goal setting in relationship and conversation with others. Remember, these are not *your* goals in isolation; your purpose is to help your church be the church.

It is part of the grace of God that we are permitted to have failures in our ministry as well as opportunities to start over. Everything you do will not succeed—nor should it. But solid, thoughtful planning—particularly in the beginning years—will help you build well and increase the ministry of your first parish.

2. The Question of Authority

ANYONE WHO HAS ever held executive office has to admire the honesty with which President Harry Truman placed on his Oval Office desk the famous sign, "The buck stops here." We seldom see such a sign on the desk in a pastor's study, for an administrative chief rarely likes to be reminded or to remind others of this discomforting fact. It is far more pleasant to try to avoid the occasional criticism leveled at you as an office-bearer when you are convinced that someone else is to blame for whatever has gone wrong. Sometimes it is tempting to think that all the troubles in your church are caused by other people with misguided attitudes, inaccurate information, vested interests, or blind prejudices. But usually the buck does stop squarely with the pastor, despite all the loopholes and inefficiencies of the democratic decision-making process. The primary responsibility for keeping your church alive and well is yours. How you work with a whole range of people and attitudes is a matter of pastoral authority in relationship to lay authority.

In addition to the official decision-making structure of your church, there exists a subtler, partially hidden power structure, which operates with minimal accountability to the church bylaws and official election process. You would be wise to identify, in your own mind, the church members who wield such subtle decision-influencing power. Considerable responsibility for the way your church either thrives or declines rests with the way you relate to these important lay persons.

Also, inevitably, there is one individual in the church who has more influence than anyone else—or so it seems to you. This person may be the one who signs the checks. Or it could be someone who so thoroughly embodies the ethos of your church that his or her word is practically law. It may be somebody who carries guilt about not being ordained and seeks to challenge and put down anyone who is. It may be the hardest worker in your church, one who has earned everyone's respect. It could be a person who cannot relate to any committee or group except as leader. Or it might be a man or woman whose character needs to question authority—anywhere and everywhere. In any case, sooner or later, you will need to come to terms with this individual who has so much authority. One of my friends calls this person the "lay pope."

When it's time to come to terms with your lay pope, keep in mind that you do not have to conquer this person in order to win your pastoral authority. The question is not which of you is the pastor of the church: *you* are. If you can enlist the willing support of this influential layperson, by being supportive yourself of her or him, you will have successfully negotiated a dangerous passage. One of the functions of the love of God is to turn potentially destructive energy to good use. It is not your personal misfortune to stumble across a threatening challenge to your authority in your church; it is simply and inevitably the nature of the institution.

At the start you probably can use some help in relating effectively to the official decision-making structure of your church. Unless you have considerable experience in the chair or good leadership training, you need to become familiar with *Robert's Rules of Order.* Your church council or a given board or committee may also benefit from a brief training session in parliamentary procedure to prevent meetings from becoming free-for-alls of discussion and generating little action. The idea is not to stifle spontaneity and good humor, but playing a football game without rules makes no sense at all.

A moderator's task is to enable the group to discuss an issue creatively and come to a voted decision. Unanimity is pleasant but not always possible, and one of your pastoral duties is to try to keep a defeated minority on board. You may be designated the moderator of a particular church committee, and in this case you wear a different hat. You may feel uncomfortable at first, especially if members of this committee are older and have had more experience with the issues at hand than you. Remember that your function is to draw their best work out of them, not to be the person with all the answers. Keep the meeting on course, clarify what is being said, press toward a vote.

Once a vote is completed, one problem that needs watchdogging is follow-through. After lengthy discussion and debate a committee may decide on a specific course of action and think the matter is resolved. A good moderator should follow up with nuts-and-bolts questions: Who is going to implement the decision? What's the deadline? If a letter is to be written, does the board want to approve it before it is mailed? Follow-through can make or break the ultimate worth of a voted decision. The vote itself is seldom sufficient.

If you are not moderating the meeting but are present as pastor, with ex officio status, this pastoral role is different from that of the moderator. You have no voting power—only voice privilege. Yet as pastor of the church, you may feel enormous responsibility for the decision under consideration and may have decided which way the vote should go even before discussion has begun. Being in such a position can be a real strain. Rather than carefully and impartially listening to expressions of opinion that are at odds with yours, you may interpret them as threats and make too much of them. Remember: Expressions of thought are only that, and an atmosphere of free expression is far better than one in which any form of repression is practiced. If your defensiveness closes you off to what others say, you might miss an important point or a valuable corrective to your biases.

A realistic way to define the role of the pastor is as resident theologian and organizational consultant. Your parishioners, with few exceptions, are very part-time churchworkers. Church is not their primary arena of responsibility, and they give it only a portion of their discretionary time and energy. You are the one person in whom the whole congregation, with its multifarious centers of concern, converges. Therein, precisely, lies your authority. The better you know your people by name and make their lives and welfare your genuine concern, the more you will in fact become a genuine pastor. The office and the authority grow out of authentic functioning. Any minister who wants immediate respect because of ordained status has failed to understand the earned nature of pastoral authority. If the people come to experience your care for them as real and reliable, they will listen to what you say, both from the pulpit and from your place at the conference table. They will not always agree with you and sometimes your most cherished ideas and plans will be shot down, but these are indications that your church is functioning as it should. Decision-making is not autocratic, and your role is that of consultant, not infallible expert.

The principal exercise of your authority is in the worship life of your congregation. To test how much the people rely on you alone for worship, watch what happens when a Laity Sunday or some other occasion for lay worship leadership comes up for discussion. There may be one or two people who would enjoy an opportunity to plan a service and even one or two who are sure they have a sermon in them—at least once—but most good Christian folk are nervous about planning and leading worship. So whether you're going to be in the congregation as a worshiper this particular Sunday or attending a conference a thousand miles away, subtle efforts will be made to involve you in the planning and conducting of the service. This has more to do with the people's need for an authority figure than with their desire to make sure you earn your salary. You are the one to whom they turn for leadership in worship, as well as the one to whom they complain if some intangible worship component seems to be missing.

More discussion about the specific components of Christian worship appears in chapter 5, but at this point let's consider the relationship of your authority to the worship experience. Unlike exercising objective impartiality when moderating a meeting, this is one area in which you are and must be an expert. You are the one who does this every Sunday, and both you and your congregation are blessed if in the process you grow in ability and expertise. The specific skill to be built and refined is your ability to enable your people to worship God together, to be an ecclesia. If over the years you become a better preacher, this is wonderful. But the body of Christ is not merely an audience who listens to good preaching; it is made up of people whose purpose is to worship, and the right use of your authority will make them stronger worshipers.

Much of what actually happens in worship is musical. Therefore, the more you know about music, the better. Some seminaries build training in sacred music into the curriculum, but usually this emphasis is lacking or inadequate. Not many divinity students choose to take it. As you begin in the ministry, you would be wise to strengthen your musical understanding and ability by taking advantage of workshops, courses, and other available resources. The musicians with whom you work need a minister who speaks their language to some extent, who can and will sing in the choir, and who is sensitive to the unique interests and problems of training a choir and continually striving to improve quality. But more than this they need a minister who can exercise genuine authority in keeping music in the proper relationship to worship. A musician can easily be tempted to fall into the trap of separating music from worship, seeing music as a distinct realm that exists primarily for its own sake. It is a specialty, and as a sphere of church life it attracts talented and creative people, who invest a great deal of time and energy in just this one thing. For them, it can become easy to consider a successful service as one in which the anthem was performed exceptionally well.

If you, as the minister, are keeping distant from this sphere of church life, you are part of the problem of segregating what should be creatively united. You are fortunate if your organist and/or choir director has had professional education in sacred music *as worship*. In most instances, the training has been strictly musical, and so you must rely on whatever the musician's previous church experience has been, together with what the two or three of you can build as a team. Don't go alone to workshops on church music; invite your organist/choir director to go with you. Perhaps members of the music committee will want to go too. *A Musician's Guide to Church Music* by Joy E. Lawrence and John A. Ferguson is extremely useful to pastors in focusing the role of music in worship, and the book should be shared with laypersons who are involved with the church's music.

Your philosophy of music in worship cannot grow and prosper in isolation. And if your organist/choir director has served in this capacity since long before you arrived, she or he will not appreciate your developing significant departures from the accepted patterns already in place. Be sure to include the musicians in your thinking and planning; encourage their contribution and attend educational events together. The goal is to plan a worship service in which the various components support and supplement one another; for example, the hymns for the day are consistent theologically, the anthem is in creative relationship with the scripture lessons and the sermon, the service proceeds logically and excitingly, and everyone is a partner in worship, with no spectators just looking on. Much of this depends on you and the kind of authority you bring to the planning and carrying out of worship. Be inclusive and collaborative whenever possible, but be firm in your expectation that worship is always the chief end. An occasional choir concert or organ recital is something quite different; Sunday services require a highly refined pastoral authority.

Closely related is the issue of weddings in the church and the music that is an important part of the wedding service. Here your authority is often crucial, because such a wide range of ideas, feelings, and expectations is operative. The organist may feel compromised by a request for music that is in bad taste or inappropriate for the organ and would deeply appreciate support from you in saying no to a particular selection. You can help the situation greatly by establishing criteria at the beginning, in the first premarital counseling session. The wedding service is a worship service—period. Its main purpose is to glorify God in the joining together of two people in holy matrimony. You will need to decide, with your organist, which type of music serves this purpose and which type does not. To separate sacred music and secular music may oversimplify the issue, because some sacred music traditional to weddings is merely sentimental, and some secular music, surprisingly, cooperates in the worship of God. If you permit music that glorifies only love in general or celebrates only the love of two people for each other, make sure such music is balanced by hymns or other components that root human love firmly in the love of God and that bring into the wedding the unique contribution of Christian truth and tradition. I am amazed at how many people want to interject all kinds of sub-Christian and non-Christian elements into the church for their weddings and yet feel strongly that the location for the service should be a church sanctuary. Living as we do at a time of rapid social change, the old boundaries between the church and the world are frequently occasions for creative conflict; sometimes the conflict only wears you down. Only you know your creative capacities and whether the requests some persons make compromise too far your duty as a representative of Christ and the church. Weddings are only one instance of such a question. In the end the issue comes down to how you bear the authority conferred on you at ordination and what you define as essential in Christian tradition.

Lest it seems I place too strong an emphasis on the autonomy of the local minister, let me put in a good word for the collegiality of Christian authority. Your duties are not formulated or maintained in isolation but rather in constant relationship with the biblical tradition, with the people of your church, with other churches in your denomination, with other pastors and theologians, with other churches ecumenically, and with the world at large. Your authority is a fascinating paradox, a continually changing mixture of personal charisma and the countless factors that shape your values in collegiality with others. Most of all, it is not your own. Pastoral authority belongs to God and is given at God's pleasure for God's purposes.

You come closest to fulfilling your calling when you serve to enable the people of your church to carry out their God-given ministry. Your authority is not threatened by a growing and improving ministry of the laity. The surest proof of your value as an enabling minister is that your people begin to care more for one another and for the poor. The true goal in fact is a church that has outgrown its need for clergy. In the meantime your purpose is to assist the church in whatever ways you can to move it toward its Christlike potential.

3. Are You a Professional?

IN AN EFFORT to counteract the effects of a widespread loss of nerve combined with a loss of confident identity among the clergy of all denominations, a movement is underway to make a side-by-side comparison between the ministry, medicine, and law, showing that ministry shares many of the characteristics of the other two disciplines and fully deserves recognition as a profession. Two books—*Profession: Minister* and *Putting It Together in the Parish,* both by James Glasse—effectively serve this interest, along with recent attempts to organize the Academy of Parish Clergy as a national association to establish professional standards and encourage higher performance levels in ministry. Many of the difficult problems of the ministry are addressed by this approach, and a good case can be made both for considering the ministry a profession and for setting uniform standards that will upgrade its general practice. In addition, one can argue effectively that certain professional disciplines, such as psychology, sociology, social work, and business administration—not to mention medicine and law—serve as excellent adjunct education and background for highly skillful ministry. Examples of ministers who have had outstanding success in incorporating two or more of these disciplines into their work come to mind.

The general lack of uniform standards of excellence in ministerial preparation is a problem; differences among denominations and differing levels of appreciation of the importance of higher education as requisite training before ordination have resulted in many different paths into the ministry. Some denominations maintain rigid requirements for ordination, including as a matter of course a bachelor's degree from an accredited college and a master of divinity degree from an approved seminary, together with supervision from a regional church judicatory or bishop. Other denominations have placed less value on educational attainments and more emphasis on conformity to a ministerial image as defined by the denominational ethos. At one end of the spectrum is the criterion of high educational achievement, and at the other end, mail-order "ordination," which admits one to the cloth simply for a fee. Down many different roads lies the privilege of having "The Reverend" before one's name, resulting, of course, in a general devaluation of the status and its credibility. Also, in the ministry are people at various levels of competency, and one can readily cite examples of ministers who exhibit impressive skill, knowledge, and experience as well as those who coast along, contributing little or nothing. Clearly, standards are lacking. This deficiency is one reason some ministers have mixed feelings about clerical status and some divinity students choose other professions. Such diversity in background and competency undercuts morale.

Sagging clergy morale is a problem that won't go away. It needs to be addressed realistically and helpfully.

But as much as I applaud and participate in efforts to raise the standards of the ministry, I am not convinced that granting it professional status fully addresses the problem or provides sufficient solutions.

Many complex factors have eroded pastoral confidence. Among them is the rapid decline of America's identity as a Christian nation. Pastoral identity is not in serious trouble within the enclave of the church, but ever-expanding pluralism and educational sophistication challenge the parochialism of any protected enclave. Outside, in the culture at large, today's minister cannot claim the social approval once current when American society knew little or no distinction between civil values and the teaching of the church. What was preached and even enforced in church was regularly reinforced at home and in school, to the extent that the Protestant ethic and the American work ethic were often indistinguishable. This association and mutual reinforcement is quickly disappearing. Had such mutual admiration never existed and had Christianity been as countercultural here as it has been at other points in its history in other places, ministers would not have become dependent on social approval for a sense of well-being and morale. But having enjoyed high status in the community—or at least living today with the memory of such a position—one is keenly aware now of the lack of it. Kierkegaard's stringent warnings against too close a relationship between church and state remain prophetic for America, despite the official separation built into the American way of life; the easiest temptations of all lure one toward captivity to the culture.

Professionalism in America is rewarded with high status and high salary or commission in return for extremely rigorous and extensive schooling and effective delivery of indispensable services to the public. A minister's education usually matches that of a professional, but the persistent fact that pastoral salaries are low, with status to match, indicates that the public does not consider pastoral services indispensable; at the point of monetary compensation the church loses most of its enclave identity and readily bases its decisions on the prevailing values of the surrounding culture. At salary decision time, lay leaders have difficulty evaluating their pastor's performance and translating this evaluation into compensation equal to that of professionals in the community with equivalent educational backgrounds and workloads. This is because the surrounding culture does not understand and appreciate the services a minister provides. Within the church itself there is ambivalence about the role of a central authority figure in an essentially democratic institution. And ministers are not adept at motivating lay leaders to raise compensation to a realistic level, partly because to do so would undercut the pastoral image of independence from preoccupation with self. The popular media is quick to expose and ridicule any minister who is "in it for the money," knowing this will touch a nerve both within and without the church. Additionally, the fact that the financial base for adequate professional-level compensation for a local pastor exists in only a small minority of churches needs to be recognized. Many churches cannot realistically afford full-time pastors even at inadequate compensation, straining the resources of fixed-income elders to pledge to a church budget too high a percentage of which is pastoral salary and benefits. Christianity never quite gets around to a radical shift toward a tentmaker ministry, although such a shift might well be a most creative change. It is resisted. One minister I know was quite willing; he even went so far as to take up an additional occupation. His church immediately gave him an ultimatum to leave the new job or the church.

To make a case for ministerial professional status is difficult for another reason as well. The question "Professional *what?*" can be asked. The medical doctor's professional service is clear and so is the lawyer's, but what does the minister do that is unique to the ministry? The eucharist requires the presiding of an ordained person in most polities, but the eucharist is, in essence, the action of the whole people of God. Preaching, while a trained specialty, can be and often is accomplished effectively by a layperson. In fact, the witness of a layperson carries a persuasive power by virtue of its totally voluntary quality. Pastoral counseling varies greatly from minister to minister in actual service rendered (chapter 7 focuses on this aspect of the ministry). Some pastors are able listeners, subtly assisting people to claim their potential and grow, whereas others use the occasion of pastoral counseling only as an opportunity to preach to an audience of one. Church administration is a pastoral specialty but, again, one that depends on adequate training and ability, and it is hardly the one factor elevating the pastor to the status of a professional. Some large churches even hire a part- or full-time business administrator who is a layperson. Taken together, the pastor's various tasks and functions add up to the practice of ministry as it is understood today, but neither together nor separately is there one compelling reason to consider the practice professional in any exclusive sense.

Ministers might be on firmer ground in considering biblical form-critical and exegetical skills a professional category. An individual who expertly develops this craft, however, is more likely to seek a seminary faculty position than a pastorate. And only some pastors understand, utilize, and develop the skill. Anyway, one would hardly advocate a return to medieval Christian distortions, in which a literate clergy is set over against an illiterate public; a laity that reads and grows in biblical knowledge is part of the strength of the church.

Returning to the assertion that a pastor is one who uniquely demonstrates the love of God in the life of a specific congregation, there simply is no professional category for this responsibility. Professional care-er, professional pray-er, and professional lover are terms that sound and are absurd.

An even more central point is at issue. The main problem with a professional definition of ministry is that professionalism is a secular-cultural category, and at its best the church stands partially outside and apart from this context. Total separation from the secular world, on the sectarian model, is neither possible nor desirable, given the incarnational basis of Christianity. But the church is a partially isolated enclave, a subculture that is losing its distinctive imperatives and character the more it blends with the surrounding culture and takes on a secular value system. Attempts to run the church as a highly refined business—complete with cost-effective studies, management training, goal-setting and achievement analysis, and credit card and automated bank transfers for pledges—fall short of the real and mysterious nature of genuine Christian community. A computerized fund transaction, efficiently up to date from a secular point of view, fails utterly to carry the symbolic power of ushers bringing monetary gifts to the Lord's Table for dedication.

The church is a hidden leaven in the loaf of secular culture, a place where a gathered community can pray, mutually, to build up the Christian faith and discover ways to bring the love and justice of God to bear on the

27

surrounding culture. Transformation of secular values rather than conformity to them, as the apostle Paul knew, remains at the heart of the Christian mandate to take the gospel into all the world.

In the meantime you and I, as pastors, struggle daily with an occupational identity crisis. Part of the crisis is clarified by comparing parish ministry with the wider arena of world mission. As long as the Christian missionary enterprise was largely motivated by the doctrinal assumption that all non-Christians were hopelessly and eternally lost unless they were led to accept Jesus Christ as savior, missions had a powerfully compelling raison d'être. But directly proportional to the increase of pluralistic values in Christianity and of toleration of divergent religious truths was a significant drop in the self-confidence of the missionary enterprise. This loss of nerve among mainline church mission work today is rationalized as emphasis on doctrinally neutral medical, educational, and political efforts to empower and liberate oppressed people. The old-style assumption that "the heathen" are condemned until they learn and own the church's point of view has become an embarrassment. The old Christian arrogance, still seen in some evangelical and fundamentalist circles, is sharply attenuated in most mainline presentations of the gospel. However, abandonment of evangelical arrogance also undercuts one of the basic motives of Christianity, like it or not. We often come close to being social workers without any distinctive gospel to communicate. Such is the price we pay for pluralism. Dean Kelley, in his book *Why Conservative Churches Are Growing,* points out that it is the incorporation of liberal, pluralistic toleration into Christian thinking that is causing the rapid decline of mainline churches. Although the point is debatable, it is one that deserves careful consideration as one attempts to identify the various causes of the erosion of Christian confidence.

One of the ways we try to avoid coming to terms with this Christian and ministerial identity crisis is to buy into the secular value system and define ourselves as professionals. To think of yourself as a professional can be tempting as the crisis makes itself felt in your bones or when a few business people in your congregation make it clear to you that they work six days a week and are puzzled about what you do between Sunday services. Try to resist the temptation. If you are faithful in your economy of time and energy to pray regularly, study hard, lead worship well, care for the sick, create the best possible sermons, counsel the troubled, delegate authority appropriately, teach confirmation class, train church school teachers, visit parishioners at their homes as well as their workplaces, meet with church committees and boards carefully prepared for their issues and tasks, involve yourself in selected concerns and organizations beyond the parish, and take adequate time for your own rest and refreshment, you need not apologize to anyone. You are following an old, strange, and entirely valid calling that is unlike any other occupation.

4. Parsonage Life

At THE BEGINNING of this chapter I use the word parsonage to mean, loosely, your personal place of shelter, whether it is a church-owned house or not. Later, the issue is examined more specifically in terms of the traditional definition of the word. Some ministers are married, some married with children, some single and living alone, some single with a roommate, and some single with children for various reasons. Probably the majority are married with children, but many of the issues discussed here apply similarly to all the different categories of ministers, regardless of whether the home is rented, privately owned, or church-owned.

One such issue is the whole question of privacy. To what extent do you want to draw a line between your public accessibility and your need for private space and time? This is not an easy question to answer, and it will come up for redefinition more than once in your career. At the beginning of my ministry I imagined a clearly defined fence around the parsonage, and only rarely and on my terms was it to be used as ministerial space. One day, on coming home after being away from town for several hours, I was shocked to find the front door ajar. One of my private interests is model railroading, a personal passion that not even in my wildest imagination had I connected with ministry; on the contrary, the hobby is a deliberate escape from ministry once in a while. When I walked into the house this day I found a man inside who had been there for longer than an hour, totally absorbed in studying my railroad layout. He had let himself in, in a dazed condition, looking for me because his wife had died just minutes before. Instead of finding me, he told me, he found a completely quiet house, where he was free to break down and cry, and then, incredibly, a miniature world into which he could escape and lose himself for a while. I was dumbfounded at the mysterious grace of God; even my supposedly private model railroad was pressed into pastoral service! My wife, Laura, and I were grateful that we had both forgotten to lock the front door.

You may imagine that you are permitted the luxury of a private self and a public self, but this is true only to a limited degree. Ministry is very much a public office, and who you are in your interior identity comes through to people more clearly than you may realize. If, for example, you seldom pray alone, all your encouragement of prayer in others has a hollow ring; your words are out of tune with your real self.

Whether you are single or married, you may imagine that sexuality is a private and personal part of your life, belonging only to your parsonage self, not your sanctuary self. But this too is self-deceiving, sometimes reinforced by a parishioner's assumption that ministers are asexual. If what you do with your sexuality is not something you can freely encourage in others, with solid theological support, you leave an important part of yourself out in the cold when you enter the sanctuary. Counseling that is built on the foundation of "Do as I say, not as I do" and conversation with parishioners in which you feel you have to mask part of yourself, again, have a hollow ring. This is not to say, of course, that you are under some strange obligation to make public all the private details of your life. However, there should be an honest consistency between your person and your work. Whether you are single or married, people notice who enters your home and take note of someone you visit exceptionally often, whatever the reason. You are a public person, and having been ordained by the church, you are accountable to the church. Many times I have heard new ministers say they are accountable only to God. God calls us to ministry, but the church confers the privilege of our work.

Clichés abound concerning the supposedly curious positions occupied by the spouse and children of a minister. Although it is neither realistic nor constructive to think of a minister's family as different in any sense from other spouses and children, the clichés persist: expectations among some parishioners that the pastor's spouse display a semipastoral eagerness to work in the church and a nearly perfect personality and never even entertain the thought of divorce, and that the children be models of decorum and maturity no matter what their ages.

These clichés exist mainly in the minds of people who live in parsonages, and for the most part, we imagine that parishioners expect such things. This could be called parsonage paranoia. Most parishioners, at one time or another, experience the enormous pressures placed on today's nuclear family, and they would have to be naive to think a minister's family is miraculously immune to these same pressures. Part of the problem is that too often we ministers perpetuate the clichés whenever we mask our actual personalities and pose as models of virtue or in conformity to whatever we perceive the norm to be. The more we are willing to risk being ourselves in public, the sooner the destructive clichés will disappear. Which is more authentically valuable: you as you really are and the members of your family as they really are or edited and censored versions of yourselves playing to a supposedly critical audience?

All this is not to gloss over a difficult problem with which each minister and family must come to terms. The problem is competition for the minister's love, which, contrary to one of the clichés, is not limitless.

When the telephone rings just as you and your family are on the way out the door to go to one of your favorite places together and it is an emergency call that requires your immediate action, you are pulled in two directions. Your capacity to love is, unexpectedly, under severe strain. Your presence and ability as a minister is being summoned. The call for help is addressed to you as a representative of the love of God—which is desperately needed at the other end of the line—your own personal compassion and anxiety are aroused, and the validity of your ministry is being affirmed in a specific instance, all of which is vitally important. But you and your family have not been out together for weeks, and you have promised them this evening, no matter what. What do you do? In most cases—and in less drastic ones too—I suspect that the minister's family members are the losers. If you are single, the issue may seem simpler; you are merely depriving yourself of something you wanted to do. This is a more significant deprivation than it seems, however. Something within you will need compensation. If you are married, the less dramatic cases are more likely to cause the most trouble. If you stop at the office en route to an evening out "just to see if Sunday's

33

bulletin came out all right," you may think it is insignificant, but as a habit, it signals something deeply disturbing to your family. No matter how much your family members seem to understand, they resent the apparent reality that they are second in your life. Some aspects of Roman Catholic celibacy realistically face the totality of God's call to ministry, for being married to a pastor is difficult. You and I need to know this and to begin right away to put our most creative energy to work on the problem. A minister's family should not always be at the short end of the stick. They deserve far better than this, and so do you.

Don't take time off; *make* time to spend with your family. Make plans with them, and enter these plans in your appointment calendar, along with the other important entries. If, occasionally, something unforeseen squeezes out your family plans, make it up as soon as possible. Your family needs you just as much as anyone else does, and more to the point, you need them more than you realize. Don't look at your family as competitors for your time and ministry. You are not their minister; you're one member of their family. They and you are severely cheated if you are absent excessively.

One of the things you and your family can do for each other is to escape the ministry now and again. Make sure you never become so ministerial that you forget how to enjoy an absolutely secular interest, or whatever activity you and your spouse and kids concoct, or how to play touch football. To get away from your pastoral role every so often and just be a member of the human race is a very healthy habit.

Friendship is another human enrichment that gets neglected by too many appointments and meetings. You are fortunate if you and another minister can become close friends—and your families too, if you're married.

Closeness to particular parishioners is inevitable but somewhat sticky if you allow it to mean too much to you; it can weaken your ministry if you become known as the special friend of a few members. But within the guidelines of impartiality you can experience warm relationships with your parishioners. Agape is one of God's gifts. Outside the church altogether, other friendships provide a much-needed diversity in your social life and a check on the development of a lopsided personality that knows nothing but church.

Now a word about the parsonage itself, in the stricter definition, as a church-owned house in which you live. As a friend of mine put it, "Living in somebody else's house is no bargain." But it is manageable and, at current interest rates, maybe the only option available if you're just starting out. As part of your church's total investment, the parsonage deserves and requires thorough maintenance and repair work if it is to maintain its investment value and if costly remedial work is to be avoided later. This calls for your cooperation with the church trustees. With their help, keep a maintenance schedule on the house, and immediately report any and all problems to them, no matter how small the trouble might be. Never put up with the irritating little problems any house develops; if you do, the trustees won't know about them until some of the little difficulties become major and expensive emergencies. You know the house better than anyone else, and the officers responsible for it have to depend on your perception and reporting. Sometimes you and your spouse may resent the disruption of your privacy such reporting entails, but it is part of your responsibility. Urge the trustees to have the house energy-audited and, if necessary, made more energy-efficient. Roof repair, tuck-pointing, and exterior and interior painting are not luxuries; they are regular necessities.

You may enjoy lawn and garden work—which can be a good hobby—but lawn mowing is time-consuming and you may want to make it part of the scheduled maintenance.

Rent-free or mortgage-free housing is a substantial monetary advantage for you at present, and one that must be reported as income on your social security forms. But remember that you are building up no equity, and whatever advantage you're enjoying now will be small comfort when you reach retirement age with nowhere to live. Unless finances is one of your talents, a good financial adviser can be of immense value in helping you to plan wisely for the future. A parsonage equity program, an individual retirement account, a loan-capable life insurance policy are all programs that, in addition to your denominational annuity participation, a financial adviser can help you evaluate and implement.

5. Worship, Liturgy, and Preaching

IF YOUR CHURCH worships well, it is fortunate indeed. Not all churches do, and their isolation from other churches and a lack of objective evaluation of worship prevents them from seeing the problem and doing something about it. In your church you are the one whose training, prayer, thinking, planning, and skill make the crucial difference between a boring hour and a deep communication with God.

Something a congregation with a history of short-term pastorates gets a little cynical about is the change in worship a new pastor can be expected to bring. You would be wise to introduce any changes gradually, but your personality may be better suited to making them immediately and getting started on developing your own style and skill. Expect some friction; from your perspective your plan is a significant improvement, but from theirs it is probably just one more minister's biases on parade. Maybe you'll be lucky and find that the plan of worship already in place is ideal—but I doubt it. Obviously, I am referring to churches whose denominational polity and order does not bind them to one fixed plan of worship but permits a degree of flexibility and local autonomy. If your denomination does bind you to a nonoptional pattern of worship, how you appropriate and interpret the components of the service matters a great deal, as well as whether you come to the task with love or indifference.

Too much popular conversation assumes that worship is, of course, boring and that a sermon—even a short one—is something to be tolerated as a nod to venerable tradition (pun intended). Such assumptions and expectations are warning buzzers, signaling that something is radically wrong with Christian worship today. To me, the worst of all pastoral sins is the thoughtless conversion of humanity's most priceless treasure into a dull Sunday morning exercise in boredom.

Actually, boredom is only one extreme to be avoided. Its opposite is a colorful extravaganza of show business that, taking its cues from mass evangelism and the electronic church, turns the people in the chancel into performers and the congregation into an appreciative audience. True worship is neither dull nor entertaining. True worship is a collective art that involves the joyful participation of everyone present. True worship converts an assembly of individuals into an ecclesia. The church, when it acts like the church, is unlike anything else on earth, and most of all, it is nothing like a passive audience. An ecclesia is a cohesive group of people motivated by the Holy Spirit to glorify God in terms of Jesus Christ.

If your congregation is to be the real church at worship, it must have an inspired pattern that every member can understand and use for participation. The worship bulletin is the basic tool for communicating this pattern. On the one hand, if its order varies greatly from Sunday to Sunday, your people cannot become sufficiently familiar with it to develop confident skill in worship. If, on the other hand, it is rigid and repetitious, you are courting boredom. What is needed is a basic framework on which your congregation can depend that permits enough flexibility and variety to keep monotony out of your sanctuary.

Have you noticed the relationship between the first eight verses of the sixth chapter of Isaiah and the currently developing ecumenical consensus in patterns of worship? A better plan, I believe, cannot be found. Compare those eight verses with these six paragraphs.

1. Coming into the presence of God is an awesome experience. The organ prelude and opening sentences of the liturgist fail if the mood they establish is not one of awe. If you aim at informality and folksiness at this point, you will initiate something other than worship. There is something deeply frightening about coming near to almighty God.

2. When humanity catches even a glimpse of the perfect glory of God, the immediate response is a humiliating sense of unworthiness: how can one survive any comparison of one's sinfulness with such absolute perfection? This humiliation is recognition of guilt and requires cathartic expression, verbally. "Woe is me!" is a spontaneous exclamation, but your people need a common prayer of confession if they are to be together at this crucial point. Some of your best pastoral work should go into composing and/or collecting appropriate confessional prayers to be included in the bulletin and prayed aloud by the congregation.

3. Confession is deeply sincere prayer, accompanied

by definite anxiety. The most threatening possibility of all is that we, as humans, may not finally be acceptable to God because of the flaws that persist so tenaciously in our mortal nature. It is your duty and priceless privilege to follow your congregation's confession of sin with a clear announcement of God's forgiveness of sin through Jesus Christ and with the gracious news that we are made acceptable by our identifying faith in Christ. You are at this moment the angel with the healing ember in your hands.

4. A community of forgiven people is in a unique position to hear the Word of God. They can hear it in the Old Testament Lesson, the Epistle, and the Gospel if these Lessons are read with consummate interpretive skill and grace. Perfect your art as a reader, and train your lay-readers rigorously. Only one's best is good enough for divine worship. God's Word is also available to the people in the text of the hymns and the choral anthem, especially when they cooperate creatively with the scripture, the sermon, and the thematic unity of a given Sunday.

5. When you preach the sermon, many different facets of the Word of God are available for refraction through the prism of your personality. Somehow God's question, "Who will go for us?" must come through what you say and how you say it. You haven't really preached until this hard question has confronted your people afresh.

6. "Here am I, send me!" is the pinnacle expression of the ecclesia. This has been the goal all along. It is a corporate "I," signifying the solidarity of a worshiping community that has been to the depths and the heights together. It is expressed in the gathering and dedication of the offering of the people and in their coming to the

Lord's Table for Holy Communion. It follows through in the outreach, mission support, and evangelism of the congregation. Worship has achieved its mark when God has been so recognized and glorified that the ecclesia positively yearns to share the experience beyond its own confines.

Liturgy is the action of the people of God that transforms an audience into a church. If prayer, the key to such transformation, is to become increasingly central in the lives of your people, they must pray together so they grow in skill and familiarity with the art of prayer. To have them listen quietly while you pray aloud is not enough. Then they are merely an audience and you are merely a performer. The real task is to enable the gathered community to pray. Some hymns are prayers. The Lord's Prayer is a direct gift from God. The people can invoke the presence of God together, confess corporately, express thanks and praise, and offer petitions and intercessions together if the worship tools enable them. Don't reserve these privileges for yourself. Make good use of the Sunday bulletin, the spoken-word sections of the hymnal and the service music, printed worship resources, and the passing of the peace of God. Also, encourage voluntary prayers from the worshipers. Above all, note how much congregational participation is built into the communion liturgy. Prayer is not a pastoral monologue, but the supreme opportunity for the church to be the church.

The best plan by far for preaching is careful adherence to the progression of the seasons of the church year and use of the three-year lectionary. Although this new, ecumenically approved lectionary is not always recognized for what it is, it does represent an enormous and unprecedented breakthrough among the separated communions of the church. Nothing less than a seedling of new Christian unity has quietly sprung up in our midst, when such widely divergent communities as the Roman Catholics, the Presbyterians, and the Disciples of Christ can base their worship on identical scripture readings on any given Sunday.

The lectionary takes the church through the Bible systematically, with an intelligent relationship of theme between the three lessons for the day. Good commentaries based on the lectionary are appearing, indicating that these thematic relationships are being explored by competent scholars from various branches of the church. Furthermore, you may gain a new or different insight into one of the lessons by virtue of its juxtaposition with the other two.

The occasional need for a topical sermon to address specifically a current event or situation, based on a biblical reading particularly relevant but not assigned by the lectionary, might be one reason for departing from the lectionary. Another reason might be a thematic sermon series extending several weeks, but even this interest can be served by the progressive movement through one book—usually an epistle—designated by the lectionary. Regular rejection of the lectionary runs at least two significant risks. One is to miss an excellent opportunity for growth in biblical scholarship and competence. Many a non-lectionary preacher selects familiar passages, deliberately avoiding those not so easily understood or appreciated. The lectionary permits you no such luxury, regularly assigning readings with which you are not well acquainted and into which you will have to dig if you are to find homiletic potential. The result can be enriching. Another risk is to work backward in sermon preparation, starting with an idea and then searching for a supportive text from the Bible. A moment's thought reveals how risky this procedure is, for all of us have known instances when biblical passages out of context have been made to serve spurious and even dangerous philosophies and programs. In twenty centuries the best preaching has always proceeded from the Bible to the pulpit, not the other way around.

If you haven't read *As One Without Authority* by Fred Craddock, and Amos Wilder's *The Language of the Gospel,* do yourself and your congregation a favor and put this book aside until you've read those two. One thing I must say here is something both Craddock and Wilder say better and more thoroughly: the gospel is so multifaceted that to reduce it to a three-point Aristotelian outline style week after week is criminal. Parables, questions, poems, open letters, impassioned speeches, narrative drama, tightly reasoned arguments, and dreams—various literary forms—all communicate the gospel in the pages of the Bible, so why restrict the modern sermon to only one classic form, practically guaranteed to bore the congregation? One hint: If you earn a reputation for being a superb storyteller, you may find that your sanctuary hasn't enough seats. It is almost a lost art. If possible, listen to Garrison Keillor, host of "A Prairie Home Companion"* on public radio, spin yarns about the lives of the folk in Lake Woebegone. The simplicity of his stories must be touching some nerves, because his nationwide audience is expanding week by week. I'm not suggesting imitation or that down-home folksiness is an appropriate preaching style or that you should aim for laughs as a regular purpose. But there is high humor in the gospel, as

---

*A Prairie Home Companion is a live radio show, created and hosted by Garrison Keillor, which is broadcast by selected public radio stations throughout the United States on Saturday evenings. It is produced by Minnesota Public Radio and distributed by Public Radio.

Frederick Buechner's book *Telling the Truth* brilliantly and sometimes hilariously demonstrates. Even more specifically, *The Comic Vision and the Christian Faith* by Conrad Hyers examines the close relationship between religion and humor. Mark tells us about Jesus: "With many such parables he spoke the word to them, as they were able to hear it; he did not speak to them without a parable [4:33-34]."

One point that may have been stressed in your homiletics classes but that, I find, may be easily forgotten is always ask yourself what you are trying to achieve with this particular sermon. A note to yourself at the top of your sermon notes could say, "The purpose of this sermon is to _____." Know your purpose and look for objective ways to find out whether or not you achieved it. Intellectual lectures may appeal to a small number; such an approach has education as its aim. Moral appeals have as their purpose duplication of your morality. Emotionally arousing presentations seek to excite and move the listeners. Each of these approaches, as a subgoal, may have a right moment and contribute to the effectiveness of your sermon. But none serves the main purpose of preaching within the gathered church; no complete sermon should use one of these approaches exclusively or have as its *main* purpose any of these three goals. Your real goal is to serve God in God's work of uniting the separate individuals of your congregation into a strong and cohesive unit, an ecclesia. Against such an ecclesia the gates of hell shall not prevail. Your parishioners ought not to leave the sanctuary the same way they entered—isolated and autonomous. At the close of worship they should be a corporate "I," glad for one another and yearning to translate the good news of Jesus Christ into their actions both as a church and as individuals.

Such a goal is high and lifted up and probably is not always achievable. It is accomplished when the service of worship is thorough and complete, touching all the bases Isaiah has given us and cognizant of the way which the church, early in its history, perfected as a plan and pattern. Genuine worship draws the people into participation in the reality and presence of God as known in Jesus Christ, so they know and feel that they have been with God for the hour. If this can be accomplished regularly among your people, you may count on God to build up the church right in front of your eyes.

6. Treating the Effects or Attacking the Cause

As ONE OF MY seminary professors used to put it, the church has always been better at organizing an ambulance service at the bottom of a dangerous cliff than at constructing an effective guardrail at the top. This may reflect the natural human tendency to wait for a crisis or emergency before taking decisive action, but I think something more is being said in the metaphor about the nature of the church. Perhaps "guardrail" is not precisely the right image, because what happens to society's victims is not so much accident usually as direct result of injustice. The people of the church—laity and clergy alike—are ambivalent about going after the root causes of social injustice and doing battle with them.

Part of this ambivalence can be traced back to the New Testament, which consistently places far more weight on the relationship of the individual to Christ than on religious responsibility to attack social injustice and institutional evil. The Old Testament supplies much of the basis for the latter emphasis. The eschatological urgency of Jesus and the apostle Paul is reflected in the New Testament so as to overshadow the imperative to transform present society here and now. Withdrawal from the world rather than critical engagement with it has often been a typical Christian stance, even though accommodation to delay of the Parousia is an essential part of Christian history.

Another part of the American church's ambivalence about social action stems from the eclipse of social vision by the predominant development of individual pietism. Revivalism has left its mark on every denomination and local church, calling for the salvation of each isolated soul but leaving largely untouched the corporate and institutional dimensions of the reconciliation of the whole creation. Sin is seen almost exclusively as personal disobedience, while institutional common cause with the principalities and powers is often only dimly perceived and named. To engage sin at the corporate level, of course, would call into question some aspects of governmental practice, business and investment factors, sexist and racist motives, industrial exploitation and environmental pollution—even a portion of the whole capitalistic motive itself. Christians in the United States are understandably reluctant to tackle the difficult issues in this arena, not only for personal reasons, but also because they feel unorganized and impotent in confrontation with such power and because the issues seem far too complex for their full comprehension. No wonder the church is ambivalent about social action. Ambivalent is the right word, as opposed to hostile, because Christians also sometimes perceive and respond to a call to attack the real causes of social injustice.

More often, of course, it is easier to organize an ambulance service after the harm has been done and to bind up the wounds of the poor and powerless wherever possible, as an act of Christian compassion. To be sympathetic healers, rather than confrontative warriors, is more consistent with the popular self-image of the church. Again, the New Testament is pressed into service of pacifistic ethics even by those who enthusiastically endorse the national expansion of military industry and the proliferation of nuclear weapons. Here the enclave identity of the church is at its most obvious, when religious values and national values are in sharp contrast and yet large numbers of people can be both patriotic and Christian at the same time. Treating the effects is more comfortable than attacking the cause. The truth must also include the confession that even treating the effects becomes unpopular when this gets expensive or demands too much time or threatens to change the relatively comfortable life of the church.

We pastors have a responsibility to keep the social dimensions of the gospel before our people in creative and challenging ways. To accomplish this difficult task, we need to be thoroughly realistic about our expectations and the actual resources of the church. When a pastor becomes angry about national priorities and directions, for example, probably the least realistic thing to do about it is to identify the members of the congregation as the problem and harangue them from the pulpit. Of course, they and you and I are all part of the problem, as democratic citizens, voters, and taxpayers who don't say *no* effectively to the sin in society. But scolding your people for decisions made in high places is far wide of the mark and does not achieve what you want it to. Too many times during the Vietnam War we pastors succumbed to the immense frustration of that era and talked to our congregations as if we were talking to the Pentagon. We vented our spleen on our listeners but communicated little or nothing to those who actually made the decisions that hopelessly escalated our country's military involvement in that conflict. We were fooled into thinking we were attacking the causes, because often what we heard from our parishioners sounded to us like support of the escalation. Scolding is not effective preaching. What were our expectations of our congregations? What if we had succeeded in persuading them that American forces should be withdrawn immediately from Vietnam? To raise this question is to turn toward realistic assessment of the resources of the church and effective leadership of these resources.

While the congregations of Christianity are not the centers of power where high-level national decisions are made, they are still a portion of the whole population and, from a biblical perspective, are leaven in the whole loaf of the culture. Therefore, part of the pastoral responsibility *is* to persuade congregations to find and express a Christian conviction on a deep social problem. But this must be done pastorally. Prophecy is Elijah confronting not a group of worshipers, but *Ahab in person*. Thank God for those denominations whose chief executives have, from time to time, spoken directly to the President and to other high officials of our government, protesting a specific policy or decision. But you and I are pastors, and our task is not to protest our congregations' views, but rather to *lead* our people in the paths of righteousness, that is, to walk with them, to understand their points of view, and to share our insights and consciences with them. We are wise to meet with our colleagues, the pastors of other churches in our community, and to work to establish a consensus among ourselves on an important issue, encouraging ourselves to lead our congregations with more strength and skill. A majority of pastors and priests speaking out together is newsworthy and persuasive. So can be even a minority. Set a realistic and achievable goal, and then look for ways to accomplish it.

In Christian efforts to influence public policy, our goal is to assist our congregations to discover the mind of Christ on a given issue and then to voice it where it will do the most good, from the strength of the Christian community. You'll never get that far if you are angry at your people and merely get them angry at you. Victory is always exhaustingly difficult, because the principalities and powers have a tenacious grip on us all.

When God says, "Who will go for us?" the question is a terrifying one. "Ahab said to Elijah, 'Have you found me, O my enemy?' He answered, 'I have found you, because you have sold yourself to do what is evil in the sight of the Lord' [1 Kings 21:20]." In the Christian response to God's terrible question is the inescapable sense of having been pursued and found, tracked down. The question is not, "Let's see the hands of everybody who would like to help us out on this." The question is rather, "Now that I have redeemed you, what are you willing to do for Me? Who will go?"

The corporate answer, "Here am I, send me!" never comes easily or lightly; it comes after wrestling, and we may well go limping. Any Christian, any human, naturally resists even a brush with a strong adversary, let alone an outright confrontation. But the strong corporate answer is, as we have seen, the end result of true worship. This is the strength you and I may not have been counting on in our fear of God's question. It is the strength the people of your congregation may not have been counting on in their experience of this same fear; we are not so different from each other, clergy and laity. It is the strength given as equipment by the Holy Spirit when two or three are gathered in the name of Christ. Suddenly, we Christians are not unorganized and our impotence doesn't matter anymore. And we go, able to do far more than we had ever imagined in our wildest dreams, through the One who strengthens us.

The actual resources of the church are far more than all we ask or think, always more than they seem. If we were to try to attack the real cause of evil with the *seeming* strength of the church—a few inexperienced volunteers, a few dollars, insufficient information, and a lot of opposition even from within the ranks—the clear temptation would be to run as fast as possible in the opposite direction. Obviously, the operative word here is temptation. And we are in fact presented with God's awful question in terms of the *seeming* puny strength of the church. Such is the test. But you and I and the people of our congregations ought to know by now how God works.

The empowerment God provides has a dark side, however. We are free to ignore God's question and call. The freedom of humanity is total and absolute. We can, in our fear of confrontation and its attendant cynicism, turn our backs on God's call and empowerment. And if such is our choice, particularly on the ultimate potential of nuclear destruction of nature and civilization, the whole responsibility is ours. Unless we do what God wants done it will not get done. Human history is not a movie, from which we can walk away at the end. If we pull the pin on this tiny garden amid the vast interstellar reaches of the universe, we cannot blame God for failing to step in and stay our hands. Unequivocally, the blame will be ours, because the stewardship was totally ours. The pastoral imperative is clearly to lead humanity to responsible stewardship of God's creation.

7. Is There a Cure in Your Office?

AN UNREALISTIC POLARITY in Christianity has separated the social and institutional concerns from the individual pastoral care, as though the two areas represent mutually exclusive disciplines and attitudes. Such polarity is reinforced in the twin distortions by which pastoral care is seen only as treating the effects of injustice and institutional confrontations are seen as outside the proper concerns of the church. To view these two areas as mutually supportive and dialectical is more realistic and constructive, all the while allowing for the variety of gifts, differences in pastoral style and emphasis, and differences in training and background for pastoral care as opposed to social ministry.

For most pastors, clinical pastoral education (CPE) is the primary training preparation for pastoral care. CPE can provide useful theoretical constructs for pastoral care, along with practical experience with hospital patients and careful analysis of the student's effectiveness as a pastor. CPE can also overemphasize the polarity between the social and individual dimensions of ministry, a bias against which the student must guard. But once you are in a full-time pastorate, CPE becomes part of the academic background, and you must now develop pastoral skills on the job. Much of your pastoral skill will be called for by the individuals who come to you with a problem that they see as personal and private. You will need to see the wider interpersonal and institutional implications of the presented problem, but of course, you start with the individual before you.

In pastoral care and counseling, two important factors can cooperate with harmful results, unless the pastor is forewarned: the intense desire of a pastor to be helpful and the natural tendency of some to manipulate the pastor. The unsuspecting pastor is looking for a clue to the person's real problem and a sign that personally applied ministry has hit the mark and is helping to resolve the problem. The counselee who is manipulative provides or withholds these clues and signs as if they were hers or his to give, as a way of gaining control of the relationship. Unless you recognize the game being played for what it is and refuse to play it, you can be drawn into a destructive relationship, all the while believing you are just doing your job. In such a game pastoral care is handicapped and may not be functioning at all.

The cycle of the game can be broken if the pastor works hard to remove one of the two factors: the pastor's intense desire to be helpful. In the final chapter I urge that you be clear about what rewards you expect from ministry. If one of these expected rewards is grateful acceptance of your pastoral care, you are in trouble. If you are to break free of manipulative relationships, you must make a conscious effort to rid yourself of this motive. To state this simply: Do not expect any stroking from your counselees. Do not allow your self-esteem to become dependent on any such support. To state this, however, is easier than to do it. The need to be helpful can mask a deeper need for affirmation of personal value—even from the pastor's own perception—unless you work at keeping clear about your motives and needs.

Everyone requires positive feedback, which forms an integral part of self-worth and emotional balance. A pastor needs objective verification of her or his effective work. The key word is *objective*. Too easily one settles for subjective stroking in pastoral counseling, in which rewards are few and ambiguous. You may counsel someone for months and see no sign of improvement or growth. But if the person keeps coming back and tells you the pastoral care you're providing really does help and is appreciated, you may be tempted to accept such stroking.for the truth. This is what you want to hear and believe. But the feedback is subjective information, similar to a patient telling a doctor that a specific treatment program is working or has cured the disorder. The doctor needs to perform certain tests before knowing whether or not success has been achieved; the patient's observation is only part of the data.

Don't let the counselee judge your effectiveness as a pastor. If the counseling relationship has gone on for a long time and your perception is that little or nothing has changed, you must make an objective decision:

1. Probably no change will be forthcoming, and improvement is not a realistic expectation; your continued supportiveness as a pastor is a positive but not pivotal factor in the person's life; or

2. Improvement of the person's situation or attitude is taking longer than you predicted initially, and some adjustment in your pastoral approach to the problem is indicated; or

3. Your expectations are off target, or you missed the most significant clues to the real issues at the heart of the problem; or

4. For a number of possible reasons you can't help and you should refer the person to someone else—another person with a particular talent or a professional counselor for a specific reason.

Each of these alternatives can be a serious blow to your self-esteem if your personal security is wrongly based on a need for positive feedback from the counselee. You must be free from such a need if you are to counsel with positive and helpful energy.

A pastor's specific and particular function is to identify the spiritual dimension of a counselee's relationships and problems, begin to channel the healing energy of God's love into the problems, and then be able to draw back and let God work. The essential point of all pastoral counseling is so easily forgotten, that our calling is to bring people to God. If you and I are too self-centered or too anxious for our own success or are misled into thinking that pastoral work is nothing more than correct application of intelligent technique, we will probably do too much tinkering, say too much, or expect too much too soon. More faith in God *on the part of the pastor* is sorely needed.

Pay close attention to the accounts of Jesus Christ's acts of curing in the Gospels. Jesus is portrayed as bringing a variety of approaches to the problems of blindness, leprosy, lameness, and other diseases of the spirit and body. First is recognition of the problem, followed by an act specifically designed for the particular sufferer, immediate disappearance of the disorder, and finally, a focus of thanks and praise to God. While pastoral care is seldom the occasion for such immediate and conclusive curing as is presented in the drama of the New Testament, this fourfold action of Christ serves as a perfect model for your pastoral work.

First, bring all the expertise you can muster to the task of recognizing the problem. But remember, your role is pastor, not psychologist. Look for the spiritual dimension of the person's problem, and begin to address it from a basis of scripture and prayer. That is, search for biblical descriptions of similar difficulties, and pray about the situation by yourself and with your counselee. The Bible and prayer are the main channels of significant insight into the problem and its resolution; without them, you and I are amateurs.

Second, shun stereotypical and packaged approaches to the person's problem. Each person is unique and special in the sight of God. You quickly lose the crucial human contact with each one when you categorize the personality and the problem. Also, you fool yourself into thinking that diagnosis is cure. The United Church of Christ has been characterized by its president, Avery D. Post, as being long on analysis but short on real help, a description that may fit other denominations as well and that certainly applies to the pastoral counseling scene as much as to social action.

Third, expect the problem to be resolved. It makes a big difference in your involvement and effectiveness whether you expect change or simply offer friendly support in anticipation of continued suffering. To be sure, in many situations cure is an unrealistic hope—terminal illness being one such situation. Your support as pastor and friend is one significant way in which God's love is available to the sufferer. Expect some kind of change, however, whether it be recovery or new strength to cope with suffering. The change as portrayed in the New Testament is sudden and dramatic, an excitement that still appeals to the "sawdust trail" sector in Christianity. But you and I are compelled to learn the art of patience. Waiting is an act of faith.

Fourth, focus thanksgiving to God, even in advance of any sign of growth or change. God can be thanked in anticipation of help as an act of faith. Aid and encourage your counselee to address thanks to God, not to you. Too many of us, clergy and laity alike, indulge self-serving desires to take credit ourselves for people's improvement, or if not that, look for subtle ways to give the impression that God makes noteworthy use of us. Give God all the credit, and make sure your counselee does too.

In short, relate to people as the New Testament suggests Christ would, in his stead and for his sake. The less self-centered your pastoral work, the less susceptible you will be to the manipulative relationship. The goal is not for you to succeed, but rather to make possible your counselee's growth in Christian faith and closer identification with the body of Christ. Healing of body and spirit does not occur in isolation; nor does it increase anyone's isolation. Enabler and sufferer are drawn closer to Jesus Christ together.

As I said earlier, if a counseling relationship has gone on for a long time with no objective signs of improvement, this brings up the possible need for referral. To whom do you refer a counselee when you have decided that someone other than yourself is needed? Not least among the options might be a suggestion that your counselee get together with a parishioner or other layperson who is coping with similar difficulties. From such beginnings are support groups built. In the first chapter I urged you to become acquainted with professional people in your community. Make appointments with directors of counseling services, psychiatrists, clinical psychologists, social workers, and other professional people to identify those with whom you might be able to work in confidentiality and trust. Again, try to be objective. Some you will like and some you won't, but this is not necessarily the primary factor. Ask intelligently considered questions that will help you determine the professional's methodology. You need to know whether collegiality is possible between you and the professional person and whether the professional is open to religious insight. You would be wise to compile your own referral notebook, based on these interviews, classifying the various professional approaches under such categories as psychotherapy, family counseling, social work, crisis intervention and emergency services, group work, adult day-care, drug abuse treatment, and alcohol counseling. You are well equipped if you know the people whose names fill the pages of your notebook and they know you.

In referral, it should be possible to bring the specialized expertise of a professional person to bear on certain aspects of the counselee's problem, while you continue to stay in touch as pastor. At its best referral is not a disengagement of yourself, but rather the bringing in of a particular kind of specialist, when necessary. The more you know of behavioral problems through education and experience, the more capable you will be of knowing when to refer; don't give in to the temptation to try your hand at analysis or therapy. For you to say, "This is a situation that calls for a professional counselor" is *not* ignorance. Were it not for your recognition of such a need, together with your efforts to persuade the person that specialized help is needed, she or he might never seek the appropriate help. Once you've made a referral, stay related yourself. If you refer someone to a cardiologist, you would not abandon the patient because you're not a cardiologist yourself!

Once you've made a referral, it is important to allow the relationship with the new counselor to become established and to mature. This process can be hindered if you remain related in a counterproductive way. Again, avoid manipulation. The person you have referred may want to come back to you and test the other counselor's techniques with you or perhaps complain that you were doing a much better job. Be especially careful at this point. You can be helpful to the progress of the counseling relationship if you do not allow yourself to be drawn into a stalemating triangle in which the person plays you and the counselor against each other. To make a referral, remain related, and yet maintain a necessary distance is not easy; this is more an art than a science and one that only you can develop skillfully for yourself.

A creative collegiality is possible between you and the professional to whom you refer, if the specialist's values are not in sharp conflict with yours. This is not to suggest that the professional must be a Christian. You should not expect the professional to become a substitute pastor; you are looking for a particular help of a kind different from the spiritual nourishment you provide. It is important, however, that the professional person not be hostile to the role of religious faith in the counselee's life. If such hostility is present, you and the professional may set up an unfortunate and unproductive conflict in which it seems to the counselee that a choice must be made between secular and religious values. This is a false dichotomy you must take care to prevent, by knowing the professionals to whom you refer.

Finally, a word about the spiritual nourishment we provide as pastors. Our dependency here is entirely on God, and it is precisely in our own vulnerability and humanity that we are most transparent to the light of God. If you seek to impress people with your skill, understanding, and strength, you are undermining both your own genuine humanity and the actual source of help. Such posturing is self-centered and therefore not of much help. Picture yourself, for a moment, as a cook at work in the kitchen, with a hungry visitor at your table. Are you so hungry yourself that you consume much of the food as fast as you prepare it, so that your guest receives only a little? Or do you partake of God's nourishment fully and regularly so that when confronted with a starving person, you can be free to give your full attention to this person and forget your own needs for a while? "In these days he went out into the hills to pray; and all night he continued in prayer to God [Luke 6:12]."

8. Relations with Other Ministers

Few GUIDELINES EXIST for dealing with the rather sensitive issue of relations with other ministers. Common sense, folkways, something akin to professional ethics, denominational barriers, jealousy and collegial cooperation are all relevant to such relationships. This factor in your life is worthy of your best thinking, for you are very much on your own in this arena. Sometimes my enthusiasm is naive. I hear ministers utter statements like, "The worst possible fate would be imprisonment with other ministers," but despite comments like this and a few unpleasant experiences of my own, I keep hoping that genuine friendship might enlighten our collegiality.

First of all, you have a predecessor. You will hear a great deal about this person from people who will always love her or him as well as from people who were glad to see this minister go. Generally, the information you receive is misleading. To join in the hero worship some express would be crippling to your own ministry; to support the criticisms you hear could be disastrous. Naturally, you want to believe you are an improvement over your predecessor, and the truth probably is that in some areas you are. But in other ways the previous minister did a better job than you will. The best policy is to let the past take care of itself and get on with the present. If your predecessor is so insensitive as to intrude occasionally, uninvited, into your new ministry, you have a big problem that needs to be resolved skillfully between the two of you—and the sooner the better. You are both fortunate if, when you do meet, friendship can be cultivated. After all, you both have a congregation in common, a shared experience of a place and people that are sacred to each of you. There is certainly no Christian reason why either should be threatening to the other, but pastoral egos being what they are, this dynamic is highly possible. The ideal, of course, is a predecessor who hopes the successor builds up the church further, and a successor who honors the legacy of the predecessor; I have seen enough examples of this kind of grace to believe that the ideal is achievable. At least we can try.

As for the ministers and priests of the other churches in your community and the rabbis of the synagogues, I have already suggested that you call on each of them right at the beginning and seek to establish a good working relationship. You are all fortunate if the local clergy association is more than just a coffee-and-doughnuts outfit. If this is all it is, see if you can help to change it. The clergy association is a first-rate opportunity for mutual problem solving, exchange of ideas, lectionary-based Bible study, issue-oriented workshops, planning for ecumenical projects and worship services, clergy retreats, and many more worthwhile activities.

Denominational differences of theology and polity are perhaps best grasped by the clergy, and for this reason you and your colleagues from other churches may have some problem areas and sharp differences of conviction between you. One clergy association I belonged to had developed the habit of poking hilarious fun at these differences, and we all enjoyed merciless ribbing. At a deeper level, the scandal of a fractured church, split asunder into competing denominations, shows up most graphically in local church relations. I hope you will look for ways to work toward cooperation, understanding, and even the eventual reunion of the separated churches.

Some aspects of your relationship with colleagues of the other churches come under the heading of ministerial ethics. Whatever you are told in confidence by or about another pastor deserves your careful protection. At some point you may hear a colleague criticized or compared unfavorably to you. Let these kinds of remarks go in one ear and out the other, and find something supportive to say about your colleague.

No pastor has any business encouraging a member of another church to change churches. This can become complicated when someone from another church starts attending yours and becomes a regular visitor. Of course, you want to be cordial and pastoral, which can come close to being inviting. If the visitor asks to speak to you and initiates the idea of changing membership, explore the person's relationship to the other church and pastor to see if a problem there might be cleared up. Otherwise, a general invitation to visitors to consider uniting with your church usually serves to help people feel welcome. The issue is a complex one, and a deft pastoral instinct will seek the appropriate ministry for each visitor. The only proper field for evangelism is the unchurched in your community.

To provide premarital counseling and the wedding service for members of your congregation is your privilege and responsibility. If such a request comes from a couple who are strangers to you, you have an obligation to inquire first into their church affiliation. If in fact they do have an affiliation, steer them gently but firmly to the church of membership. A moment of truth may ensue. They may have already attempted to secure the services of another pastor; in many such instances one or both persons are divorced and are members of a church that prohibits remarriage. Their minister or priest is strictly forbidden by denominational law to provide the marriage service. You must decide whether or not you and your church can be of help in such a situation. If you frequently agree to marry people with this particular difficulty, you will surely begin to establish a reputation among the rapidly growing divorced population. That such couples will unite with your church is unlikely, and for you to encourage it would be unethical, as we have already discussed. With rare exceptions, such a couple simply does not desire a civil ceremony and looks to your church strictly as a religious place where they can marry. Perhaps you view this use of your services as a temporary but valid ministry to strangers with a real problem, but I have difficulty with this concept. Christian marriage is distinguished from marriage in general by several significant theological characteristics, not the least of which is the grounding of marital love in the community of faith. We seriously compromise and dilute the Christian witness when we provide wedding services that have no relationship to our own congregations; in such a situation the church building is only a wedding chapel. This is an issue for thorough discussion between you and your deacons or church council.

Returning to the question of whether the couple has already sought the services of another pastor, it may be that the other pastor, for a reason other than denominational law, has refused to provide the marriage service. In this case ministerial ethics clearly requires that you contact the other pastor and weigh his or her compunctions carefully. It may be a denominational factor that is not relevant to your denomination or it may be a serious impediment that the other pastor discovered. Extended premarital counseling on your part might eventually help to clear up such a problem. You may deem it best, however, to stand with the other pastor in refusing to officiate.

If the couple has not sought the services of another pastor and has no active church affiliation, you are on more solid ground. Again, I am wary of an attempt to use my church as a wedding chapel, but here is a valid opportunity to become this couple's pastor and to begin to include them in the life of your congregation. This should be the basis of your counseling with them, whatever else you decide is necessary to explore in their relationship with each other.

Sooner or later you may become part of a staff. Usually, a church of more than four hundred or five hundred members is too great a responsibility for one pastor. In such a case, the pastor may be joined by a copastor, an associate pastor, one or more assistant pastors, a director of Christian education, or one or more student assistants. Each of these categories has its own particular set of dynamics built into the relationship. Because the emphasis of this book is on the beginning years, it is realistic to think of you as an associate or assistant pastor. The church that calls you to such a position will have some guidelines established, perhaps by previous experience or by the present perceived needs of the church and requirements of the senior minister. Making sure these guidelines are clearly understood by everyone—you, the governing board of the church, the other pastor(s), and the members at large—is extremely important. Your job description could well make up the whole agenda for at least one church council meeting. To whom are you directly answerable? What should be done if additional duties start getting tacked on? What exactly is expected of you? What are your expectations and goals? To have a distinct set of responsibilities that are yours is best, rather than a vague and general plan to divide the tasks of ministry casually or situationally. The quality of your relationship with the other minister(s) on the staff depends on the clarity of these guidelines and the way in which they are accepted and understood. Again, I want to emphasize the importance of friendship. One of the games some churchpeople play is to try to set one minister against the other and to form competing loyalties. This can be a tempting trap for you, especially while you are getting started and building up your personality in the ministry; if you aren't careful, it can feel very good to allow people to affirm you and to put down the other pastor(s). At best, this is a dead end; at worst, it can be the seed of a horror story. Ministerial ethics help, but the best defense against such a trap is genuine, supportive friendship between staff members.

I have mentioned that you have a predecessor. Although it may seem a bit premature to bring it up here, from your first day in your new parish you are becoming someone's predecessor yourself. Eventually, you will have a successor.

When this time comes cut the pastoral ties with your congregation and move on. No matter how much some wish you could still be their pastor and will always look at you this way, that your pastoral role and identity in this congregation begin to fade is crucial for both you and them. This will be painful for you and the people of the congregation; they will feel abandoned, and you may wonder how anything real can be temporary. This is one of the mysterious paradoxes of our vocation and, in a larger sense, of the ambiguity of the human condition itself. One minister I know, who has felt keenly the pain of separation from a former parish, says that once you have met people in the deep places of life you have met forever. I believe that only in the kingdom of God can some of the temporal and geographic disruptions of human love eventually make sense, that unity can conquer isolation completely, that death can be swallowed up in victory. Perhaps you can find a graceful way to continue various relationships on the level of friendship, but do all you can to guide former parishioners to accept their new pastor *as pastor*. Another aspect of the paradox is that if former parishioners feel that suddenly you no longer care about them, this can work to undermine their trust in the new pastor; they will wonder if she or he will become cold and aloof. Of vital importance is that you do everything in your power and understanding to provide support for the new pastoral relationship of your successor.

One of the best ways to provide this kind of support is by staying away. Don't return to your former church unless you are specifically invited by your successor and then only if it seems right from as many angles as you can see. If a former parishioner contacts you and asks you to come back to provide a pastoral service because of a particularly close relationship, you should gently guide the parishioner toward the new pastor and communicate with your successor about the request. After consultation, your successor may think it appropriate for you to come back in response to the request, and in this case, you might agree to assist your successor. But do not make yourself available for continued pastoral services or encourage former parishioners to turn to you. Get on with your new responsibilities; don't live in the past.

As the years go by you will develop certain attitudes about relations with other ministers and build into your practice the various aspects and necessities of ministerial ethics. There is a hard way to learn these things, and I don't recommend it. Too much harm can be done by ministers who are casual about collegial ethics. To give the whole issue your best thinking, from the first day on the job, is by far the better way. As I have said, there are few guidelines on this issue—at least of the kind that get written down and codified; mostly you pick them up as you go along and work them out for yourself.

9. *The Greener Pastures Myth*

I DON'T BELIEVE any pastor ought to stay in the first parish for an entire career. Some instances come to mind in which a one-parish career has been effective, but rare is the church and minister that can stay together for a long time and remain fresh and vital. But I do believe some common ministerial assumptions about moving need careful examination. Sometimes a kind of wanderlust sets in and one dreams of being elsewhere, not because the present parish is a painful place to be, but more because of an essential rootlessness. Sometimes a pastor feels he or she has achieved all it is possible to achieve in this parish and experiences a desire to move on. Or sometimes a first-parish experience teaches a pastor a great deal about himself or herself, and the need for more specific training or a need to specialize becomes pressing. Unfortunately, in other situations the relationship between pastor and congregation has deteriorated to the point of pain, and one senses a strong need to escape. In all these situations some common assumptions about moving are operative. Whether or not you ever identify exactly with any of these situations, a time will probably come when you will utilize the appropriate denominational channels to send out a signal that you are available for a call to a new place. When this time arrives you will have reached a crisis of one kind or another, and your best thinking may be short-circuited by emotions.

If the crisis is such that you have reached the limit of your effectiveness in your first parish, to move may be appropriate—but not necessarily. You should consider other options. Have you talked it over with your regional executive? He or she is your pastor and also has pastoral concern for your congregation. The insight of your pastor may be what you need to gain a new perspective on yourself and your parish.

Have you sat down with your lay leaders and honestly worked hard together to solve the problems of the parish, as *you* see them? We pastors spend so much time and energy on problems as our parishioners see them that sometimes we leave our viewpoints and feelings out in the cold. Many times we fail to share our own personalities and problems with our lay leaders, believing such conversation has no value, without ever trying it. Your regional executive might also be able to play an important role here, meeting with you and your lay leaders, together or separately, to help initiate new directions and understandings.

Have you thought about a sabbatical or leave of absence or talked over this option with your lay leaders? Perhaps what you need most is a radical change of pace and emphasis and a refreshing distance from the day-to-day life of your parish. A sabbatical can be an excellent opportunity for pursuit of an advanced degree, for taking a complete course in an area in which your background is lacking, or for engaging in extensive analysis of your career with a career professional. One cautionary word about sabbaticals: Some churches have granted their pastor a sabbatical only to be presented with a pastoral resignation at its end, and having this kind of story on the grapevine may make your lay leaders nervous about considering a sabbatical. To use a sabbatical to search for a new job is bad ethics. Your church deserves a promise from you that the sabbatical will be used to strengthen you for your present job.

One reason I urge consideration of these alternatives to resignation is this: Part of the problem is you, and you take this part of it with you wherever you go. Leaving your first parish does not solve that part of the problem; it merely relocates it. Your first parish is probably the best place to begin to address any flaws in your leadership style, when they begin to surface.

Another reason I urge consideration of alternatives is that part of the problem is your church, and it needs all the help it can get at this critical time. Bringing in the denominational regional executive while you are still there can be a positive step to take.

You and your church might reach a surprising breakthrough in understanding and positive energy if you're willing to try, and a new chapter in your ministry can commence right where you are. Adversity is one of the masks opportunity wears. Your resignation closes the door to the mutual growth of your first parish and you. Only you can decide whether it's finally right to close this door, but don't make this decision without seeking all the available help and counsel.

One of the unexamined assumptions we carry around is the greener pastures myth. We think if we could just leave where we are and be lucky enough to be called to a larger, or wealthier, or more prestigious, or more liberal, or younger, or more appreciative, or more energetic (you fill in the description) church, we could be the minister we were meant to be. Part of the illusion is to view the present parish as unable to make use of our talents and as restrictive and spirit-dampening. The illusion is compounded whenever we visit other churches and find highly creative projects in progress, sanctuaries and facilities that make ours seem small and poor by comparison, or situations that appear strongly supportive of the pastors—greener pastures, in other words. These findings makes us want to cross over to the other side of the fence.

Or we think if we could leave the parish life altogether and work at a higher denominational level, our real abilities would be tapped and we would discover the real action. The attraction to the other side of the fence or the next rung up the ladder is a myth that disappears like a mirage once we have actually made a move, only to resurface as a lure to the next horizon after the new job becomes familiar and its conflicts begin to emerge. This is pure escapism, and an illusion that seems to fool every one of us. I know of only one ordained person who deliberately sought a move from a highly prestigious position to a poverty-stricken, Third World parish. Most of us succumb to the success-spiral motive and either wish for or consciously seek greener pastures.

Rarely is a minister's first-parish salary adequate. Making ends meet is a harrowing experience that gnaws at you day and night. A small or large increase offered by a second parish is tempting by comparison, and it may look like a substantial gain. But this too is part of the illusion. The salary-parsonage package provided by almost every church places every minister in a difficult position relative to the cost of living, particularly at retirement age when she or he has accumulated no equity. The rewards for being a minister are certainly not financial. For us to face this fact and not let ourselves be seduced by the illusion that somewhere in the future lies a comfortable economic security is important. Earlier I referred to the tight financial resources of the small, struggling church. Given the fiscal and budget-setting realities of most local churches, it is unlikely that the ministry in general could ever become a financially secure calling. But we have also looked into the captivity to the culture that affluence can bring with it, so our ambivalence continues. It is sometimes argued that the best way to free a minister from undue preoccupation with money is to provide adequate salary—and I tend to agree—but we must be realistic about the source of the salary and not gain it at the expense of other crucially important items in the church budget. Again, I am driven to the concept of a tentmaker ministry, a subject to which I turn in the next chapter.

One encouraging sign is the gradual leaning toward the practice of a church selling its parsonage and getting out of the housing business. Some advantages such as property tax exemption and the capability to offer a pastor free housing, are forfeited in this decision. But much is to be said for the idea. The housing portion of the church's budget can go instead into pastoral salary. A higher salary, no tax exemption, build-up of equity, and personal responsibility for home maintenance puts the pastor on an equal footing with the parishioners. Also, the parishioners' illusion that free housing gives the pastor a big financial break is eliminated; this is of vital importance, because this illusion is one of the main reasons why pastoral salaries are kept low. Gaining equal footing with the laity in the community, as a homeowner and property taxpayer, can only increase the pastor's credibility. As long as we clergy are viewed by parishioners as being protected from the harsh realities of life, what we say and do carries less weight. Also, if you own your own home, you may be less likely to move for the wrong reasons.

To say how long you should stay in your first parish or second parish or any parish is impossible. This answer varies with an infinite number of important factors. I am urging you to consider your option *not* to leave when leaving becomes an almost irresistible idea. One chronic weakness of many local churches is that, at any given moment, they are adjusting to a new pastor. The conventional wisdom is that at least three years are required for this adjustment to be made. It can easily take this long for the new pastor to get to know the people of the parish and for the people to come to understand what the pastor expects of them and what he or she can be expected to do. Once these mutual learnings have had time to mature, effective teamwork can get underway.

If you leave your first parish before you've been there three years and the church calls a new pastor, it will experience at least five or six weak years while trying to understand and adjust to leadership changes. One might say that much of the church's hesitancy, ambivalence, and loss of nerve, which I examined in an earlier chapter, is caused partly by the high turnover of clergy constantly searching for greener pastures. We pastors can do our part to help strengthen the life and work of the church by staying where we are and giving that parish the best of which we are capable and by not giving in to the siren calls of escapism.

10. Tentmaking

After this [Paul] left Athens and went to Corinth. And
he found a Jew named Aquila, a native of Pontus,
lately come from Italy with his wife Priscilla, because
Claudius had commanded all the Jews to leave Rome.
And he went to see them; and because he was of the
same trade he stayed with them, and they worked, for
by trade they were tentmakers. And he argued in the
synagogue every sabbath, and persuaded Jews and
Greeks.

—Acts 18:1-4

AN EARLIER PASSAGE in Acts (6:1-6) sug-
gests in rudimentary form the ecclesiastical separation of
clergy from laity, a distinction that has managed to create
as many problems as it solves. In the multifarious institutional forms and expressions of Christianity only a small
number of Christian communities have been clergy-less.
From the beginning of the church, usually apostolic authority has required—or at least implied—a full-time
commitment to leadership that excludes any competing
obligations to another occupation. The church consistently holds that all its members are called of God to live
the gospel of Jesus Christ and to minister to people in his
name, but that some are to forsake any secular occupa-

tion and income and to devote themselves entirely to leadership of the church.

Apparently, Paul knew little of this distinction in any formal or legal sense. He was quite willing to take time for earning daily bread and for the other necessities of life by secular occupation and commerce. Indeed, for Paul, being financially independent and self-sufficient was more than merely an option he had chosen; it was part of the foundation from which he preached the gospel: "For you remember our labor and toil, brethren; we worked night and day, that we might not burden any of you, while we preached to you the gospel of God" [1 Thess. 2:9].

The early days of Christianity, of course, were far less institutionally formal than the church of today, and one can argue that Paul was not strictly accountable to a local church or an ecclesiastical authority in the same way a modern pastor or priest is. In some ways he was a first-century equivalent of an interim minister; or if we base our portrait of him on Luke's description of his life-style in Corinth, he comes across as an articulate and persuasive layperson. Luke shows us a tentmaker who makes apostolic use of the sabbath—at least in one scene.

Those primitive Christian conditions cannot be reclaimed, nor can modern times be made over in the image of the first century, as sectarians sometimes wish. But one can recognize in Paul a personal independence from the finances of the church that modern ministry does not know. Does it make any sense to suggest that ministry today might be strengthened by a similar independence?

The question mark is deliberate, for this is more a tentative exploration of the issue of tentmaker ministry than a definitive set of conclusions. Maybe the answer to this question is no, but I believe both sides of the issue need to be examined: one, whether the quality and authority of ministry is strengthened by a voluntary rather than compensated commitment on the part of the minister, and two, whether it is the best stewardship for a small church with limited financial resources to put the highest percentage of its budget into pastoral remuneration.

Let's look at the first side of the issue. In a recent informal meeting between the diaconate of my church and visitors desiring to become new members, we were going around the circle telling what had first attracted each of us to this particular local church. When it was my turn one of the deacons interrupted and said, "*You* came because we paid you to come!" We laughed, of course, but because the statement is partially true, it undermines some essential qualities of ministry. I say *partially* true, because I am in my present pastorate for a whole collection of reasons, not the most important of which is the amount of remuneration. But that I could not have come to this or any church without a salary is also clear.

Or could I? As long as we assume that the pastoral ministry must be full-time work with full-time pay, we never ask this question. Creative energy of a strange and unfamiliar kind begins to flow if we refuse to indulge this assumption. The traditional pastoral duties listed at the end of chapter 3 become impossible to perform if the pastor can give only part of his or her time to the church. Obviously, if each of these tasks is somehow essential to the meaning and well-being of the Christian community, Christians will see to it that one way or another they get done. Equally obvious, the most popular way to cover the list of duties is to contract with an ordained minister who agrees to do these tasks on a full-time basis. Laypersons feel they do not have the time, the expertise, or always the inclination to do the things they expect their minister to do. To me, time seems to be the main factor. If an ordained minister had to spend the greater portion of daylight hours earning an income by secular work, the primary anxieties of this minister and congregation would be that many important tasks were not being done and that their minister was not immediately available on call. Such anxieties could not be sustained for long; quickly a unique covenant between the minister and the people would be necessary in which the responsibilities of the minister and the responsibilities of the people would be clarified and accepted. The minister might be surprised at how many pastoral tasks can be accomplished in spare time, and the laity would discover unexpected talents among themselves that formerly they had thought of as ministerial.

The most significant change would occur in the nature of the minister's accountability to the congregation. Under present conditions and arrangements, the congregation's primary leverage can be the power of money; when the people are paying the bill, they are entitled to demand satisfaction on their terms. This puts the matter coldly and crassly but also brings it into sharp relief. The businesslike purchase of a minister's services is light-years away from the apostolic motives portrayed in the New Testament. Our pastoral credibility is always undermined by the suspicion that our real motive is our salary, a suspicion that heightens as the salary increases; witness the skepticism with which the well-dressed electronic-media preachers are regarded by all except their most devoted fans. Lenny Bruce used to say that any minister who owned more than one suit while some people are in rags is a phony. The absence of an ecclesiastical salary totally removes this ground of suspicion and can help restore to the ministry its authentic apostolic motive and credibility. While a person might seek a pastoral position for a whole cluster of reasons other than the apostolic imperative—such as a need to be in a position of leadership or a personal need for a pulpit from which to speak—once the financial factor is removed, at least that motive need no longer undermine the pastor's credibility.

The worker priest movement in the European Roman Catholic Church has served to explore another aspect of priestly or pastoral credibility and, in a similar way, so has the experience of many small black churches. When the pastor is a worker in the marketplace or factory, like the members of the congregation, the people can be sure their pastor knows intimately and firsthand exactly what their daily lives are like. Unless the pastor is one of them, they can never be sure he or she knows what they're talking about when they speak of the grindstone, unions, taxes, bosses, payroll responsibility, conflict on the job, and the hundreds of other concerns that occupy the waking and sleeping thoughts of workers. When the pastor is in the same boat with everybody else, everybody else knows they've got a genuine sister or brother: a model provided for us in the incarnation of Jesus Christ, who, in the words of the United Church of Christ Statement of Faith, "came to us and shared our common lot."

Turning now to the second side of the issue, to consider pastoral salary as one item in the total church budget and to raise the question of stewardship are important. To be sure, many—if not most—laypersons and ministers would not want to rock the boat to the extent that I am rocking it, preferring to keep the ministry a paid position. And much is to be said for this. Again, I am not advocating any conclusions but rather exploring the issues.

Is it the best stewardship of Christian resources to put the largest percentage of local church money into pastoral salary? Apart from building maintenance, utilities, and insurance—which is a whole subject in itself—most small churches *primarily* support a pastor with the money available for use. Maybe the overwhelming weight of tradition and custom argues that this is good and realistic stewardship. But one has to wonder what else a church might be freed up to do if this burden were off its shoulders. Scholarship funds, grant and loan programs for specific needs, low-cost housing construction, food and fuel bank support, gifts to colleges and seminaries, local church support of denominational and ecumenical projects and missions, new ways to serve handicapped and homebound people, child and adult day-care are just a few items taken from a long and exciting list of creative things many local churches already do but currently with only the smallest portion of the church budget. Think what could begin to happen in communities, nations, and the world if these creative ideas and projects started to receive the *primary* budgetary emphasis! The heart always follows the treasure, and I am beginning to think that a tentmaker ministry just might help to unlock a vast Christian potential that has been only barely glimpsed.

What else could a minister do to earn a living and still be a pastor? If the truth were known, I think every minister asks this question again and again, more in terms of an alternative to the pastorate than as an adjunct. When the question is framed in terms of an alternative occupation, often negative dynamics are operative: one thinks of leaving the ministry, radically changing one's identity, trying to understand how still to be faithful to the call of God, trying not to feel like a failure, and so on down the gloomy list. But when the question is put in terms of an adjunct occupation, these negative dynamics need not cloud the issue at all. A pastor can look positively and creatively at a broad spectrum of occupations, many of which are well-suited to his or her abilities and interests. Full-time or substitute teaching, human service work, further training for a specific field, sales work, manual labor, and development of a small business are some possible occupations for part-time pastors. I have always wanted to open a model railroading shop and raise Irish setters when I retire, but why should these possibilities necessarily have to wait until I retire?

Prophets of doom who love to predict that the church is on its last legs in human history refer to a tentmaker ministry as a coming economic necessity. Pastors will be forced, they say, to moonlight at first and later to earn all income from secular employment, because the church can be expected to dwindle further and further in people and resources. I don't believe this. I suggest instead that a tentmaker ministry might be one live option for building up the church that so far has been generally overlooked. At the very least, this idea could inspire the kind of diaconate and church council discussion that opens up Christians for creativity and courage.

11. Burnout

ONE OF THE realities in ministry or human service work of any kind is the experience of a unique type of fatigue, one that differs from the normal tiredness after exertion. The deeper we reach into the human condition and the harder we have to work at helping to meet the real needs, the more likely we are to know this fatigue. Yet it cannot be emphasized strongly enough that this is not the same as simply being tired; we are dealing here with a tiredness that relaxation and sleep do not cure. This fatigue can be likened to a terminal disease, and it is called burnout. It is a matter of giving more than you receive, until finally, you have little or nothing left to give. It is a disease of the spirit, the symptoms of which can go unrecognized and untreated for years, unless you train yourself how to spot them right from the beginning of your ministry.

Recently, I attended a lecture on burnout in the ministry, and I went through my usual self-defensive reaction as the speaker described the progressive stages and symptoms: "Oh well, that will never happen to *me*." This is like applying the statistics about heart disease to everyone except yourself. I was startled out of my isolated smugness by the speaker's well-documented assertion that burnout happens to one hundred percent of us in the ministry, and that all of us are already in at least the first of three progressive stages.

I remember well a bad moment I had during my first year in the ministry. My exuberance at finally having started in my vocation was chilled for a tick of the clock by an older denominational executive who told me it is quite possible to approach retirement feeling cheated by a vocation that never turned out to be what you had expected. This comment suddenly started a new train of thought in me, one that gains strength with the passing of time: We must be absolutely clear about what we *expect* from the ministry as a career. A whole cluster of unexamined, disguised, and buried motives and needs require an honest examination in the light of day. I am not referring to psychoanalysis or even the kind of self-probing that is pushed in Clinical Pastoral Education. These approaches to problems may be valuable under certain circumstances, but what I am suggesting is simpler. Regularly ask yourself what *you* expect in return for your service as a minister. And be clear and honest with yourself and others about whether you're getting it or not. Only you know what your real expectations are, even if you have to work to uncover them; other people's expectations of you must be separated out if the question is to receive a true answer. What do *you* expect for yourself, from the ministry?

Meeting the challenges of a whole career and reaching retirement without feeling cheated seems, to me, to have much to do with receiving—seeing to it that throughout your career you keep receiving what you need most. My assumption is that giving is not at issue. If you are not constantly giving to people, you are in the wrong vocation. Based on the crucifixion, the true apostolic motive is to give Christ to people. Giving is the essence. But you might not be receiving enough and not even know it. Symptoms of burnout usually go unrecognized. Steeped as we are in a religious ethos that canonizes martyrdom, we can be tempted into a kind of masochism that misses the good news. While we are called to take up the cross and follow Jesus Christ, we must be reminded that only the cross of Christ can save the world, and we are witnesses to this truth. Any follower's attempt to climb up on his cross serves no good purpose whatever. Yet we can be tempted to give masochistically or, conversely, to deny ourselves the nourishment we need as though we were not entitled to it.

Four factors play into this denial of our needs. First, the pastoral self-image is that of giver. To be a receiver falsely carries an implication of weakness. Second, it can be terribly hard to ask for help, especially from parishioners and colleagues. Rather than a simple appeal for help, this request can feel like an admission of ineptitude. Third, study of the Bible and prayer can become so thoroughly our vocational skill that we seldom just read the Bible and pray for the spiritual experience itself. Similarly, we too need to hear good preaching from a voice other than our own. Fourth, we probably do not make good use of our denominational executive in our genuine need because of this person's role in our career advancement and our unwillingness to make what we suppose would be a bad impression. In short, when you add up these four factors, we are not good receivers. And when the well is not fed by deep springs, eventually it dries up.

Burnout is deadly for both the church and the minister. It sneaks up on both, unobtrusively. The syndrome of unawareness, protectiveness, familiarity, and laziness often keeps the church or the minister from doing anything about it. Over the years the creative cooperation of clergy and laity is gradually eroded; no one actually misses what might have been, because no sharp contrasts bring the matter into focus. The result is a minister who keeps putting up with a job that is not fulfilling and a church that keeps putting up with a minister who does not lead. The unspoken resentments on both sides, if brought to the level of conscious recognition, would be enough to create a volcano.

What can be done about burnout? The first step in the right direction is to recognize it as both an occupational hazard and a disease. Recognition comes first; without it we don't know anything is wrong. Once burnout is seen for what it is and is named, for lay persons to blame it entirely on the pastor or for the pastor to assume the whole burden of guilt for it is inappropriate. This is not a simple case of pastoral irresponsibility, but rather long-term, subtle erosion to which ministers are particularly vulnerable. If the minister's needs have never been identified or met along the way or have had their legitimacy as needs denied, burnout eventually takes its toll one way or another. Feeling cheated is one way. Losing faith is another, in which the grace the pastor preaches sounds hollow, because the pastor does not experience it. Withdrawal is another way; it becomes easier not to risk rejection of one's pastoral leadership by offering it less and less. Cynicism is perhaps the worst way of all, in which everything is finally relativized and rationalized away.

Another step is to learn how to become a better receiver—right now, in your first parish. Read the Bible and pray, apart from sermon and worship preparation, so you stay in communication with God yourself. Look at

Moses, *receiving*—not creating—the Law. Look at the prophets, *receiving* assurance that God would be in their words and deeds. Look at Jesus, repeatedly seeking God in prayer. Look at the apostles, *receiving* Jesus' promise that he would be with them always.

Get to know your regional denominational executive as a friend, so when you find it necessary to turn to this person for help with a problem, it will not be your only relationship. One of the executive's responsibilities is to be there to help you when you need it, not to judge you unfavorably because you need it.

Don't be afraid to trust your people with *your* perspectives on church problems; their perspectives can weigh too heavily on us and drown ours out. You cannot expect the people of your church to understand you and help you if you never give them a chance. The walls will not cave in if you confide in your people that something is bothering you or that you need them.

Insist on a sabbatical, study leaves, vacations, and available educational experiences, such as workshops and conferences. An objective distancing from the daily intimacy of your ministry is a healthy move, from which you will return refreshed and newly informed.

And get away from it all, regularly. Do the things you most enjoy doing or, if you're married, the kinds of fun families invent together. Don't feel guilty about this or apologize for it as if you were taking something that doesn't belong to you. Sometimes more than one day off a week is exactly what you need; many weeks will go by when even one day off will seem impossible, but that's workaholism or mismanagement of time or both. Claim some time for yourself.

Most important, take the responsibility for your own career. There are usually many complaints about inefficiency with any denominational placement system, whether episcopal, presbyterial, or congregational. The expectation seems to be that the placement and advancement system should be a service which is well acquainted with each pastor and caters efficiently to his or her individual needs. No such system is possible, of course, no matter what the polity or skill of administration. Pastors who expect to be known automatically and sought out for significant jobs and recognition will be sorely disappointed. This kind of disappointment leads directly to an attitude of self-pity, which is at the center of the disease called burnout but is hidden or disguised as something else. Make up your mind what you most want to do in your ministry and where you want to do it. What are your actual talents and where does God lead you? What credentials do you already have and what others might you need to obtain? Do you seize the best opportunities for service that come through the mail and over the telephone? Do you make yourself available for denominational work beyond the local level? Do you see your relationships with other ministers in the community and the clergy association as opportunities for new ideas and cooperation? These are some of the ways you can be called to service and new growth. Seek the guidance of God for the shape and substance of your ministry, and then go after it with single-minded determination. Don't wait for the placement and advancement system to discover you; take all the responsibility yourself for the kind of ministry you intend to provide. It has been said that seminary students are typically passive. One of the cutting edges of the transition from seminary to parish ought to be the outgrowing of passive behavioral modes. If you are passive about your career, you are a prime candidate for burnout.

Switching from one denomination to another, like changing parishes, does not solve the passivity problem.

For other reasons perhaps you are more at home in a different polity and ethos, but usually the attractiveness of another denomination is merely one more aspect of the greener pastures illusion. Unless your theological and ecclesiastical convictions are against the grain of your present denomination, it is probably better to stay where you are and work out your ministry in the ethos you know best.

Something in me other than self-defensiveness still wants to do battle with the lecturer mentioned at the beginning of the chapter. Burnout, he contends, happens to one hundred percent of ministers. Even if statistics support this conclusion—which I'm not sure they do—I have known enough older ordained people, and laity as well, whose Christian light still shines, to convince me that burnout doesn't have to happen. I think of an old woman in Kansas City whose theology was sharp and whose love was pure health. I will never forget the long-retired minister in Chicago who helped me to stop wavering and take seriously the call to the ministry by saying, with tears in his eyes, that no amount of money could buy the richness of his pastoral experience. I still count on the supportive example of a retired denominational executive in Massachusetts who will never stop loving people with something like Christ's love. I think of the minister honored in Connecticut for fifty years of pastoral service who responded with the most stirring statement about ministry I've ever heard. I think with gratitude of a host of laypersons who have stayed with the church through long lifetimes and have kept giving it their weathered best, no matter what. Burnout does not have to happen.

One final word about receiving: It is standard behavior for clergy to remember Jesus' teaching that it is more blessed to give than to receive. But there is another statement in the New Testament, from Paul; that we should mark and remember equally well: "I delivered to you as of first importance *what I also received* [1 Cor. 15:3]." There is no hint of burnout in the church's hardest-working apostle, perhaps partly because Paul knew he was not the originator of the gospel he transmitted. You and I may not be so clear on this point, half-believing that everything we do with and for people has to come from ourselves and our own resources. This illusion is a killer. You and I are receivers of the grace of God, as was Paul, and as much as is the parishioner whom you have such trouble liking.

It is this grace alone, not your self-generated energy, that makes the difference between life and death. When we have grasped this portion of the good news, we can see that we clergy can be, quite literally, saved.

Suggested Reading

Buechner, Frederick. *Telling the Truth: The Gospel as Tragedy, Comedy, and Fairy Tale.* New York: Harper & Row, 1977.

Carroll, Jackson W., and Robert L. Wilson. *Too Many Pastors? The Clergy Job Market.* New York: The Pilgrim Press, 1980.

Craddock, Fred B. *As One Without Authority.* Nashville: Abingdon Press, 1979.

Dittes, James E. *Minister on the Spot.* New York: The Pilgrim Press, 1970.

Edelwich, Jerry, and Archie Brodsky. *Burnout: Stages of Disillusionment in the Helping Professions.* New York: Human Sciences Press, 1980.

Fray, Harold R. Jr. *Conflict and Change in the Church.* New York: The Pilgrim Press, 1969.

Fuller, Reginald H. *What Is Liturgical Preaching?* London: SCM Press, 1957.

Glasse, James D. *Profession: Minister.* Nashville: Abingdon Press, 1968.

————. *Putting It Together in the Parish.* Nashville: Abingdon Press, 1972.

Harris, John C. *Stress, Power and Ministry.* Washington, DC: The Alban Institute, 1977.

Holmes, Urban T. III. *The Future Shape of Ministry.* New York: Seabury Press, 1971.

Hulme, William E. *Your Pastor's Problems: A Guide for Ministers and Laymen.* Minneapolis: Augsburg Publishing House, 1967.

Hyers, Conrad. *The Comic Vision and the Christian Faith: A Celebration of Life and Laughter.* New York: The Pilgrim Press, 1981.

Jud, Gerald J., et al. *Ex-Pastors: Why Men Leave the Parish Ministry.* New York: The Pilgrim Press, 1970.

Kelley, Dean M. *Why Conservative Churches Are Growing.* New York: Harper & Row, 1972.

Kemper, Robert G. *Beginning a New Pastorate.* Nashville: Abingdon Press, 1978.

————. *The New Shape of Ministry: Taking Accountability Seriously.* Nashville: Abingdon Press, 1979.

King, David S. *No Church Is an Island.* New York: The Pilgrim Press, 1980.

Lawrence, Joy E., and John A. Ferguson, *A Musician's Guide to Church Music.* New York: The Pilgrim Press, 1981.

Mickey, Paul A., and Robert L. Wilson. *Conflict and Resolution: A Case-Study Approach to Handling Parish Situations.* Nashville: Abingdon Press, 1973.

Moberg, David O., *The Church as a Social Institution.* Englewood Cliffs, NJ: Prentice-Hall, 1962.

Nouwen, Henri J.M. *Creative Ministry.* New York: Doubleday, 1971.

Oates, Wayne E. *Confessions of a Workaholic.* Nashville: Abingdon Press, 1978.

Oswald, Roy M. *Crossing the Boundary Between Seminary and Parish*. Washington, DC: The Alban Institute.

———. *The Pastor as Newcomer*. Washington, DC: The Alban Institute, 1977.

Ray, David R. *Small Churches Are the Right Size*. New York: The Pilgrim Press, 1982.

Schaller, Lyle E. *Parish Planning*. Nashville: Abingdon Press, 1971.

———. *The Pastor and the People*. Nashville: Abingdon Press, 1973.

Schmidt, Elisabeth. *When God Calls a Woman,* tr. Allen Hackett. New York: The Pilgrim Press, 1981.

Stewart, Charles W. *Person and Profession: Career Development in the Ministry*. Nashville: Abingdon Press, 1974.

Wilder, Amos N. *The Language of the Gospel*. New York: Harper & Row, 1964.